MAC KING'S CAMPFIRE MAGIC

FOREWORD BY PENN & TELLER

ILLUSTRATIONS BY BILL KING

BLACK DOG
& LEVENTHAL
PUBLISHERS
NEW YORK

Library of Congress Cataloging-in-Publication Data available upon request.

Published by Black Dog and Leventhal Publishers, Inc.
151 West 19th Street, New York, NY 10011

Distributed by Workman Publishing Company
225 Varick Street, New York, NY 10014

Printed in the United States

ISBN: 978-1-57912-829-6

© **Mixed Sources**

Product group from well-managed forests, controlled sources and recycled wood or fiber

FSC www.fsc.org Cert no. BV-COC-080720
© 1996 Forest Stewardship Council

TABLE OF CONTENTS

BECOME YOUR OWN ROADSIDE ATTRACTION

By Penn & Teller

There are three attractions we always tell our friends visiting Las Vegas to be sure and see: Hoover Dam, the Liberace Museum, and Mac King.

Hoover Dam is as big as the Pyramids but a lot more useful. The Liberace Museum tells the story of a pianist who proudly wore rhinestone capes and conquered the world. And Mac King's show—well, it's like Penn's mom's sweet-milk biscuits or Teller's mother's roast pork: the best in the world.

Mac does "Comedy Magic." But don't picture a loudmouth using magic to make fools of people. And don't imagine some clown pulling out rubber chickens and screwing up tricks. Mac's tricks are beautiful, funny ideas—amazing things that turn your brain so far inside out that your only option is to laugh. And even though he's fooling you, you don't feel foolish. You feel as though he's giving you a gift. He's your friend, doing something for you, not to you.

We just pulled a standard magic book out off our shelves and saw instructions for making a handkerchief appear under a soup bowl. Now think about it: If you had real magical powers, would you use your paranormal abilities to stick snot-rags under plates? We certainly wouldn't. But magic books are full of such stupid stunts. That's not what you'll find in *Campfire Magic*.

Here you'll find strange, mysterious things that will make your friends laugh and gasp. Some of the tricks are entirely Mac's genius (for example "Get a Life," where you seem to make a live plant grow from a seed stuck in the ground only seconds before). Some are Mac's clever adaptations of pointless old tricks (turning a knife into a fork) into astonishing new ones (make a dry stick sprout leaves).

Mac's designed these tricks to be done on camping trips, on picnics, or if you get shipwrecked on a desert island. Now, some of the pictures show campers in uniforms, like the kind worn by organizations that wouldn't want Penn & Teller as members, but don't let that scare you. You don't have to wear a ranger hat, a kerchief, or a green outfit to do these tricks. You can do these in your pink pajamas. You can even bring many of them right into your own home, as long as your grandmother isn't too nervous.

There is a kind of wickedness about all magic tricks. You are, after all, lying to your audience. And normally lying is bad. But magic is a good, honest wickedness. Honest, because your friends know you're doing a trick. Good because you're not taking something from them, but giving them something: a moment where their brain lights up and does a crazy dance.

Before we send you off into this book, here's a tip: If you can find a friend to study this book with, you'll be able to help each other. You can take turns being magician and audience. You can catch each other's mistakes and practice together. Take it from Penn & Teller: a magic partner is a good thing to have.

So go forth and bring good wickedness to the world. For, thanks to Mac, you can now make magic in your own back yard.

INTRODUCTION

Howdy, I'm Mac King, and I'd like to welcome you to *Campfire Magic*. It is my firm belief that nearly everybody likes a good magic trick. It's also my firm belief that everyone ought to know at least one cool trick or stunt. Therefore I've rounded up all sorts of awesome tricks for you to learn. There are amazing tricks to do when you're camping, astounding tricks to do at your scout meeting, shocking tricks to surprise your friends, and hilarious tricks to play on your parents. And even if you don't want to learn a magic trick, there are funny stunts, skits, gags, and practical jokes, too.

I also believe that doing magic is good for you. And that's just what you should tell your parents when they hassle you about doing your homework instead of practicing a magic trick. Tell them that you're becoming a more interesting and well-rounded person, because that's really the truth.

And speaking of practicing your tricks, I'm sorry to say that there's really no such thing as a trick that takes absolutely no practice. Happily, though, none of the tricks in this book are the kind that you have to devote a lifetime of study to master. There are tricks here that range from the ridiculously simple to the somewhat difficult, but thankfully none that are ridiculously difficult. Remember, though, that just because the trick seems simple doesn't mean it's not a killer trick. Some of the best tricks in the world are also the least difficult.

Magic doesn't have to be hard to be good; as a matter of fact, I happen to think it shouldn't be hard. The best magicians I know are the ones who really love the time spent amusing themselves by practicing and polishing a new trick; it never seems hard to them because the process is so much fun. As you get better at it you may want to tackle some tricks that take more time, effort, and skill to perfect. However, my thought has always been that if it seems like a horrible chore to learn a more complex trick, then it's probably best for you to stick with the simpler ones (or take up a different hobby). If you just like the idea of learning a few clever, funny stunts and that's as far as you want to take it, I'm fine with that. The idea is for you (and your audiences) to have fun!

Even though many of the handsome illustrations in this book depict me wearing a scout uniform that doesn't mean you have to be a Boy Scout to do any of the excellent tricks I explain here. So even if you're not a Boy Scout, or even a boy for that matter, I hope you'll find something here that you'll like.

From the desk of Lewis T. Monkey

As a monkey assistant of some renown, I'm often asked by fans what I would consider the key to my ever growing popularity and success. I generally reply that, while I'm regarded as pretty easy on the eyes, my real skill is adaptability. "And where did I hone this skill?" my madding throngs of admirers invariably rejoin. "Scouting!" I respond in a hale voice and a flourish of my willowy arms.

Yes, as a young monkey in the lush overgrown forests of French Guyana, I, Lewis T. Monkey learned the secrets of adapting to its often brutal environment as a member of Chimp Scouts troop 477! I also learned to appreciate the vast wonder and beauty that surrounded me. These secrets of adaptability were life lessons that carried and protected me along my journey to Sunny Las Vegas and into the employ of its most beloved magician, Mac King.

What is the connection between scouting and magic? Well gee... we're just full of questions today, aren't we? I suppose a scout must be alert and always aware of what is happening. A scout that is easily fooled is a danger to himself or herself and the troop at large. Conversely, a scout who can fool others will likely be a great success. Most importantly a scout must be entertaining. It's no fun to be stranded in the wilderness with a bunch of bores. So learn some Scout Magic and you might just be spared the task of fetching water or heavy tent poles. Yes, you'll be much too valuable to troop morale to be stuck with such menial tasks.

In conclusion, I feel that, in many ways, I owe a debt to scouting, and that combined with this country's deplorable chimp-labor laws has made my complicity in the compiling of this tome both rewarding and mandatory. So please enjoy.

Lewis T. Monkey

MAGIC RULES

Just so you know, there aren't actually any rules as to how you become a magician. But I do have a few suggestions. First, decide which trick you want to learn. You can look at the list of tricks in the front of the book and pick out something because you find its name intriguing, you can flip through the book and select a trick because a particular monkey drawing made you laugh, or you can simply start at the very first trick in the book and work your way systematically from the front of the book straight through to the back.

Once you decide which trick to learn, begin by gathering up the necessary props. There's nothing required for the tricks in this book that you shouldn't be able to find in your knapsack, desk, or kitchen, so that should be an easy task.

Once you have all the props required, read the directions carefully. I've laid out each trick step-by-step. When you feel like you can visualize what the trick is supposed to look like to the audience (in magician lingo we call this "the effect"), then try going through the trick with the props. If it works, great! If it doesn't quite come off perfect, don't panic; sometimes it takes a few run-throughs before everything clicks. Re-read the directions, maybe you forgot a step; each step is important, and if you leave something out, the trick probably won't work right. And be sure to pay attention to the fabulous Bill King drawings, they help make this learning process a zillion times easier.

Once you've gotten the trick to work, go through it a few more times in private, until you're sure about every step. For some tricks it's a good idea to practice in front of a mirror so that you can see what it looks like to your audience. If you have a video camera, it can be a wonderful tool to help you practice. Do the trick for the camera and then go back and watch it. You'll get good even faster this way.

Once the trick looks decent to you, it's time try it on someone else. This is where it helps to have a monkey assistant. If you don't have a monkey, you can use a close friend. Before you do the trick, explain to your friend (or monkey) that this is something new you're working on, and you want him to watch you do it and tell you what he thinks. Do the trick and then really listen to what your friend says. If he is a true friend he will kindly tell you if the trick looks right or not. If, on the other hand, your friend watches your trick and laughs and points and is mean to you, maybe you should stick with the monkey.

Once you've tried the trick a few times for your friend, and feel like you've got it, feel free to spring it on anyone you can con into watching. That's really the only way to get good at being a magician—you have to do tricks for people.

When you're performing for people here are a couple of tips. . .

It's a good idea to not tell your friends how the tricks work. Unless you want to. That's right, there's no law that says you can't tell your friends the secrets behind the tricks. BUT, because the secrets are so diabolically simple, your friends will almost certainly be bummed out that they were so easily fooled, and they may not want to watch any more of your tricks.

It's usually a bad idea to do the same trick twice for the same people. A big part of any magic trick is the surprise. The second time you perform a trick for people you lose that element of surprise; they know just what to watch for, and that makes it easier for them to catch you.

For the same reason, don't tell your audience what you're going to do before you do it. That's nearly the same as doing the trick twice. You've given them an idea of what to be on the lookout for. That's almost always a bad idea.

Don't worry about being nervous. I can remember when I first started doing tricks for people I was so scared I could feel my knees shaking in my pants. Even now, when it's a really important show, like when I was on *The Late Show with David Letterman*, I still get anxious. But the thing that helps you get over being nervous is confidence. And there are two main things that'll help you beef up your belief in yourself. First, the more you practice a trick the more you'll feel certain you can pull it off. And second, the more you perform a trick for people the more you'll realize you've got what it takes to do this magic stuff.

And finally, remember to have fun. If the audience senses that you're having fun, they'll have fun too. If you seem relaxed, it relaxes the audience. And a relaxed audience is easier to fool!

ROPE TRICKS

Scouts have a reputation for knowing a lot about knots and ropes. There are lots of great books on how to use rope to tie an assortment of useful knots. This book shows you how to use rope for a much more practical purpose-magic!

Before we get going, a quick word about rope. The best rope for most of these tricks is soft cotton clothesline. Sometimes what you find in the hardware store is pretty stiff because it has starch in it. If you run that rope through the washing machine it'll come out soft (uncoil the rope and put it into one of those mesh laundry bags that are used to wash little delicate items).

Just ask whoever does the laundry at your house for help. If you're going to use the same piece of rope over and over, you'll probably want to dip the ends in white glue and let them dry. This will keep the ends from fraying

We'll start with a really simple but effective one....

KNOT SO FAST

What They See

Scouts are known for their knot tying ability. In this trick you tie a knot so fast, it must be magic!

Holding one end of a piece of rope in you hand you bring the other end up to your hand as you cryptically announce, "On the count of three."

Counting, "One," you release one end of the rope. Nothing.

You bring the end of the rope back up enclosing it in your fist and then release it again on, "Two." Still nothing.

You bring the end back up into your fist, and then say, "Three." This time, as you release the end of the rope a nice tight knot has been magically tied in the end!

What You Need

✔ A piece of rope 20-30 inches long

What You Do

I hate to disappoint you, but before you show the trick you need to tie a nice tight knot in one end of the rope. Hold that end in your fist with the knot concealed by your fingers (see ❶ for a super-secret exposed view).

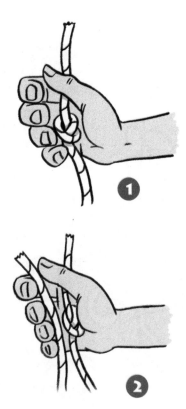

Exhibit the rope to your audience, making sure that no one can see the knot. Announce, "On the count of three," as you bring the bottom end of the rope up into your fist alongside the top (knotted) end (see ❷ for another exposed view). By saying, "On the count of three," without saying what will actually happen on the count of three, you get people curious about what's about to occur, without giving them something specific to watch for.

Counting, "One," you release the untied end of the rope.

Again, bring the untied end back up alongside the knotted end. Say, "Two," as you release the untied end once more.

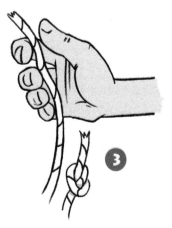

One last time, bring the untied end back up into your fist. This time, as you say, "Three," you secretly release the knotted end of the rope so that it looks as if a knot has instantly appeared on the end of the rope!

BE PREPARED

You can have the rope with the knot already prepared in the end concealed in your pack or coiled up behind some other prop so that no one can see it (and yet it's easy to get to) and pull the rope out with the knot already concealed. And don't forget, you can also use a neckerchief, handkerchief, or bandana for this when no rope is available.

So that's a super-simple way to make a knot magically appear in a rope. Next is one that takes a bit more practice....

KNOT AS FAST

What They See

Draping a length of rope over your hand you give a little turn and flick of your wrist and –ka-pow!– a knot appears tied in the middle. While this is really a flourishy demonstration of skill and not a magic trick, it will definitely enhance your reputation as a nimble-fingered wonder-worker.

What You Need

✔ A piece of rope about 20-30 inches long. The piece you used in the previous trick is perfect.

What You Do

Begin by draping the rope over your right hand. The rope is not draped evenly. The longer end "A" hangs across your palm and then goes between your pinky and ring finger. The shorter end "B" is held in the crotch of thumb and hangs down the back of your hand. Check out ❶ to make sure you're holding it right.

    Rotate your right hand palm down, turning it inward toward your body, making sure that the shorter end of the rope ("B") swings in between the longer end and your body.

    Grasp the shorter end ("B") between your index and middle fingertips ❷.

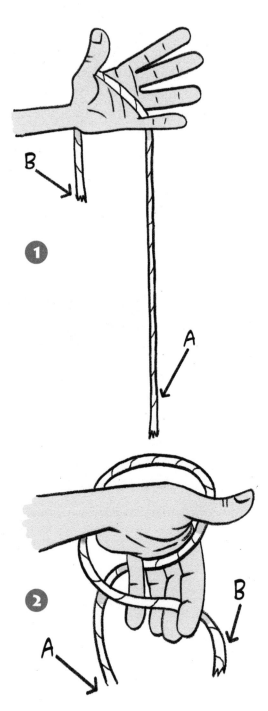

Keeping a firm hold on the end of the rope with your index and middle fingertips, give a quick downward and then upward flick of the wrist. The part of the rope draped around your hand will drop off, producing a knot! ❸

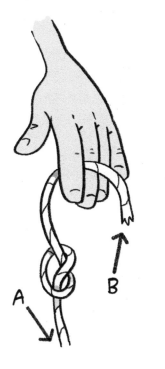

A ↙   B ↗

❸

BE PREPARED

There is a certain knack to doing this that you can only get by trying it a few times, but once you understand what's happening this is really much easier than it appears to the impressed onlookers. I will admit, though, that sometimes I have to flick my wrist twice to get the rope to drop off my hand. But even when I have to resort to a second flick it still looks great.

It is a good idea to learn a few tricks and stunts like this one that look really difficult.

Any time you do something that is obviously based solely on skill it enhances your reputation, and makes people more likely to give you credit even when the trick you're doing doesn't require any dexterity at all.

It's also a fine idea to study a few stunts that enhance your reputation for having mysterious and strange knowledge of odd information. Like this next little challenge. . . .

KNOT SO SIMPLE

What They See

Laying out a piece of rope in front of his unlucky chum, the magician claims, "Any scout worthy of the title should be able to grasp the ends of that rope, one in each hand, and tie a knot in it without letting go of the ends of the rope." After the pal makes a number of unsuccessful attempts, the magician makes good on his boast.

What You Need

✔ A length of rope 20-30 inches long

What You Do

Invite someone to help you. Stretch the rope out in a straight line on the ground (or table) and issue the challenge stated above. Make it seem like a test of great importance. Give your participant a few chances to do it. Unless he knows the secret already there is no chance he will stumble upon the solution. What you're going to do is, in effect, tie a knot in your arms and them transfer that knot to the rope.

When you think the time is right (before everyone gets too bored or too frustrated) you do the following: First, cross your arms as in **1**. Then grasp one end of the rope with your left hand **2**, and then the other end in your right **3**. Keeping a tight grip on the ends of the rope and your arms crossed, stand up. Pause so

that everyone can see the situation. Don't let go of the rope, but slowly uncross your arms . When the arms are uncrossed there will be a knot right in the center of the rope!

BE PREPARED

As the audience member is making his useless attempts to tie a knot, other spectators will begin to offer advice and maybe even want to try. If this isn't a formal show, but just a group of people hanging out, there's no harm in letting anyone else who wants to give it a try. You might even want to have a few extra pieces of rope so that a number of folks can have a go at the same time.

Keep in mind that this can also be done with a piece of string, a bandana, neckerchief, or even a cloth napkin. Simply grasp the cloth at opposite corners, one in each hand. Swing it like a jump rope. This will twist the hanky (or whatever you're using) into a kind of loose rope that is ideal for this feat.

HOW TO CUT YOUR SCOUTMASTER IN HALF

What They See

With the aid of two other scouts, the magician cuts the scoutmaster in half by pulling two ropes right through his body!

What You Need

✔ Two ropes, each about eight to ten feet long
✔ One piece of thread the same color as your ropes
✔ At least three spectators

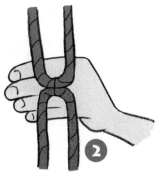

What You Do

There is a tiny bit of advanced secret preparation you need to do before the trick can be done. First fold each piece of rope in half. Then, tie the centers of the two ropes together using the piece of thread. Trim the ends of the thread close to the rope ❶. If you grasp the ropes in your hand, hiding the thread joint, it looks like two ropes run through your hand ❷ for a close-up view showing the ropes in your hand). Place the ropes somewhere you can reach them easily, making sure that the tied centers are hidden from the audience's view, but easy to get to. You're ready to cut someone in half.

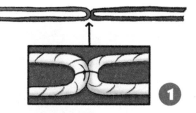

Begin by announcing that it's time to cut the scoutmaster in half. Have him stand facing the audience. Invite two other audience members to help you. Have them stand facing the audience on either side of the scoutmaster. They should each be about three feet from the scoutmaster and about two feet in front of him. ❸ is a handy diagram showing where everyone should be standing.

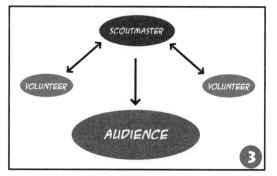

Bring forth the ropes holding the joint concealed in your right hand (check ② again) saying, "Because a saw is much too bloody and horribly painful, we'll be using these two ropes to cut right through the middle of his body." Look at the scoutmaster and say, "Don't worry this method hardly has any blood or pain."

Stand between the scoutmaster and the volunteer on his left and, using your left hand, give the two ends of the rope to that volunteer. Keep the right hand closed around the joint in the two ropes. ④ shows this action from the audience's point of view.

Step behind the scoutmaster, and using his body for cover, transfer the thread-tied joint in the ropes from your right hand to your left.

Continue moving to the right to a position between the scoutmaster and the volunteer on his right. Keep your left hand (the one with the center of the ropes) behind the scoutmaster while handing the remaining two ends of the rope to the other volunteer using your right hand ⑤.

Ask the two rope holders to step back to take up the slack in the ropes. As they move back, your left hand continues to hold the center of the ropes behind the scoutmaster's back.

Once the ropes are stretched out straight (careful that they don't tug too hard or they'll break the thread holding the centers of the ropes together), you let go of the centers of the ropes and walk around to stand in front of the right-hand volunteer. The joined centers of the rope remain hidden behind the scoutmaster.

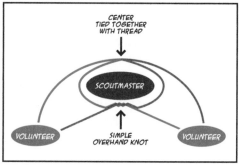

Ask each of the volunteers to hand you one of the ends of their ropes. It doesn't matter which end they give you. As you say to the scoutmaster, "I know this is a scary situation for you, and I don't want you to run away, so we'll tie you in place," tie a simple single overhand knot with the two ends the volunteers gave you. Give the ends of the rope back to the volunteers. Make sure the left volunteer gets the rope you were given by the right volunteer and vice-versa.

This subtle exchange of ends happens naturally when you tie the overhand knot. It also secretly brings both ropes to the front of the scoutmaster's body. Everyone but you thinks both ropes are behind the scoutmaster. **6** shows the true situation from above.

Remind the volunteers to hold on tight to their ropes. Tell the audience that on the count of three the volunteers will pull on the ropes and both ropes will pass from the back of the scoutmaster, through his body, and end up in front of him, thus severing his body completely into two pieces!

Count slowly and clearly, "One, two, three, pull hard!" When the volunteers pull hard on the ropes the thread holding the rope centers together will break and both ropes will wind up in front of the scoutmaster , seemingly penetrating right through his body!

BE PREPARED

 This seems a bit complicated to read, but it's really pretty simple when you actually try it with the ropes. The only real problem is it takes three additional people to practice this trick. So to sort of get the general idea of how this works you can try it using a chair back as the scoutmaster and have one friend playing the part of one of the volunteers, while you play the part of the other volunteer and the magician.

When this is part of a longer show, every so often throughout the show I'll announce to the audience, "And coming up, don't forget, we're going to cut Mr. Jackson in half" (obviously you'll substitute the name of your scoutmaster—or whoever you plan on cutting in half). This really builds up interest and gets people excited.

PSYCHIC LARIAT

What They See

A long piece of rope is first examined and then you begin coiling it up. The spectator is given a pair of dice and asked to stack them one on top of the other. You finish coiling the rope and drop it on the floor. Then you have the spectator add the numbers on the three hidden faces of the dice—that is, the top and bottom of the lower die and the bottom of the upper die. When the spectator uncoils the rope it is seen that a number of knots have magically appeared tied along its length. Amazingly, the number of knots matches the number chosen by the spectator. The rope is psychic!

What You Need

✔ A pretty long piece of rope (about 20-25 feet, or so)
✔ A pair of dice (you can take them from a board game)
✔ A table or other flat surface on which to stack the dice

What You Do

Before we get into the trick itself, let's have a little dice lesson. Did you know that the singular for "dice" is "die"? And did you further know that every die has six sides and the numbers on opposite sides of the die always add up to seven? We're going to exploit this seven thing in order to learn what number the spectator chooses. If you stack one die on top of the other, three of the 12 numbers are hidden. During the trick, the total of those three hidden numbers will be the spectator's chosen number. Since the opposite sides of one die always add up to seven, it stands to reason

that the opposite sides of two dice will always add up to 14. Duh. So if you stack one die on top of one another you will know that the three hidden numbers will be 14 minus whatever number is showing on top of the stack. ❶ shows you what I'm talking about.

Now that you have some clue as to how you know the chosen number, I'll describe how to magically make the right number of knots appear tied along the length of rope as we go through the trick step by step.

First, bring out the rope. Hand one end to someone and have him tug on it. Ask him to make sure that there are no knots tied in the rope. This allows the audience to come to their own conclusion that the rope is free from trickery, and is much better than saying, "I have here an ordinary length of rope."

Next, bring out the dice and have the person roll them a few times to make sure they come up different numbers. While he's rolling the dice you start coiling up the rope. But you have to do it in a special way so that knots will form when it's uncoiled.

Start with the rope stretched out on the floor. Drape one end of the rope over your left hand so that about 16-18 inches hang down behind the back of your hand. Clip the rope in the crotch of your left thumb ❷.

Grasp the rope with your palm up right hand about 15 inches from your left hand.

Turn your right hand over as you move it up to your left hand. This will make a single tricky loop that you hang on your left fingers. I call this a "tricky loop" because if you did this correctly, you'll see that the long end of the rope is hanging behind the loop. ❸

Your left hand keeps it's grip on the first loop as your right hand repeats its actions and forms a second loop, ❹

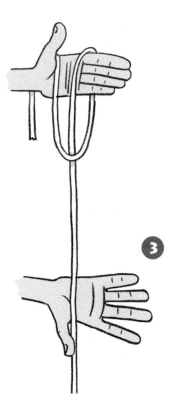

3

4

25

placing it in the left fingers next to the first. Again, make sure the long end of the rope is behind the loop you just made.

As the spectator is checking out the dice you make eight of these tricky loops. Eight is the smallest number that can be on the hidden dice surfaces (14 − 6=8).

Ask the spectator to stack the two dice one on top of the other while your back is turned. Tell him to let you know when he's done the stacking. When he announces that he's done, turn toward the spectator and say something like, "There are three hidden numbers in that stack: The top and bottom of the lower die, and the bottom of the upper die. When I turn away from you I want you to add up those hidden numbers. Please don't say the total out loud until I ask you." Turn away from the spectator and say, "Go ahead and add those hidden numbers together." What no one knows is that when you turned toward the spectator and explained about the hidden numbers you were also taking a sly look at the number on top of the stack and subtracting it from 14 to give you the chosen number. Very sneaky.

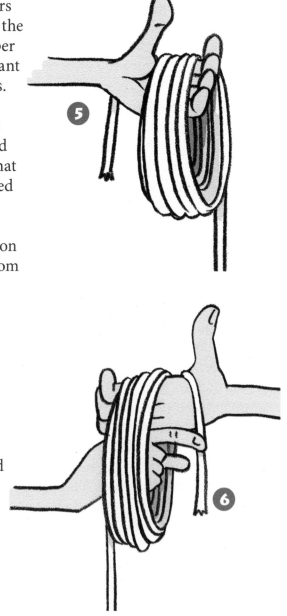

While he's adding up the hidden numbers, you make however many more tricky loops you need to bring the total of tricky loops up to the chosen number. For example, if you saw a two on the top of the dice stack, you'd know that the secret number was 12, so you'd need to add four more tricky loops to the eight you've already made.

When you're finished making the loops, your left hand will look like ❺. With your right hand reach through the center of the loops and

grasp the end of the rope that's been
hanging over the back of your left hand
6. Pull this end back through the
center of all the loops **7**.

Your right hand keeps
its grip on the end
as your left hand
carefully lays all the
loops on the ground
(notice in **8** how
the end held in your
right hand goes through all the tricky
loops down to the bottom of the coil).

Ask the spectator if he has the secret total. Tell him to
announce it in a loud voice.

Since the tricky part is all over, now is a good time to build
up the trick a little bit. Remind the onlookers that they looked
over the rope and it didn't have any knots in it. Tell them
that the rope was on the floor before the secret number was
announced. Make sure they understand that what is about to
happen is a miracle.

Once they understand that what
they are about to see is impossible, you
can give the people some reason for what is
about to occur. You can say that the rope came
from a psychic's clothesline and seems to have
absorbed some of her psychic ability. Or you can say
that you are a psychic magician and can mysteriously
cause the rope to tie itself into knots with your brain.
You can make it funny or serious.

Once you've done the hype, now it's time to deliver.
Repeat the chosen number so that you're sure everyone
heard it. If someone didn't hear the total then
they're not going to be impressed by what
happens next.

Your right hand still holds the end
of the rope. Slowly lift that end up
as you gently shake it. As you keep
lifting higher a knot will emerge from

the coils. Loudly count "One." **9** shows this first knot emerging. Keep lifting higher, gently shaking, and another knot will appear, "Two." Keep lifting, shaking, and counting knots out loud until you've lifted as high as you can. At that point, hand the end from your right hand over to the assisting spectator saying, "Here, you take this end, and slowly back away."

You re-grip the rope just above where it is emerging from the coil and continue lifting, shaking, and counting. Try to make the counting build dramatically to the last knot. When the last knot emerges, grasp the end of the rope that still lies on the floor and stretch the rope out between you and the spectator. With this impressive pose the audience should applaud wildly!

BE PREPARED

The goal is to finish making the loops and have the coiled rope on the ground before he even knows the total of the secret number, but don't worry if you don't make that goal, the trick is still really strong.

As the knots emerge from the coil it is possible that the rope will get a snag in it. Usually the gentle shaking you're doing as you lift the rope will prevent that problem, but if the rope does become tangled, you can usually fix it by using your left hand to undo whatever small jam has occurred.

I first learned this trick in a book called *Learn Magic* by Henry Hay. It's a mighty fine book, filled with wonderful advice, and is still available.

Don't forget to put the dice back in the Monopoly game.

CHAPTER 2

THE GREAT OUTDOORS

Most of the tricks in this book can be done equally effectively inside (say, at a friend's house or at a scout meeting) or outside at a campsite. These next tricks are all ones that *must* be done outside.

GET A LIFE

What They See

You plant a seed in the ground and make a real live plant instantly grow by magic. It's supernatural!

What You Need

✔ A small plant about seven to nine inches high growing outside in dirt (not grass) with no other plants growing within 12 inches of it
✔ A seed or bean

What Really Happens

Once you've found the correct size plant, dig a hole about 10 inches long and one and half inches deep right next to it **1**. Gently fold the plant down so that it lies in the hole **2**. Cover the plant with the dirt you dug up **3** trying to make sure it looks just like the surrounding area. Put a small pebble or stick in the ground at the base of the plant as a marker so that you'll know where it's buried. Put the seed in your pocket.

This trick is best when you're walking around in the woods (or your backyard) and you "suddenly get an inspiration" to do a trick. Just make sure inspiration strikes you when you are standing right next to the spot where you've buried the plant (that's what your maker is for).

"Hey, the other day I found a strange seed," you say as you remove the seed from your pocket. "I wonder what kind of plant would grow if we planted it?" you ask as you kneel down in front of the buried plant.

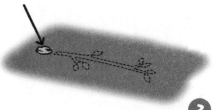

"I've been experimenting with a super-fast growing method. All you do is plant the seed in the ground about one inch deep," you say as you show the seed again and push it into the dirt at the base of the hidden plant.

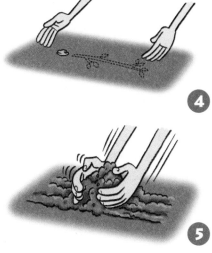

"Now we just need a little spit." Spit on the spot you planted the seed.

"And now the key ingredient—dirt massage," you say as place one hand where the top of the plant lies buried under the dirt and your other hand the same distance from where you planted the seed ❹.

"That's right, dirt massage," you repeat as you bring your hands together above the base of the plant, scooping up the plant and as much dirt as your hands can hold ❺. Be careful not to uproot the plant. You're basically just unfolding the plant under cover of the dirt in your hands.

Gently rub your hands together as you say, "The massage really speeds up the growing process." Keep rubbing your hands together, but let the dirt slowly escape between your fingers little by little revealing the plant ❻. You've created life!

BE PREPARED

If you're uncomfortable using spit, as a substitute you can either sprinkle a little water on the ground or use some magic growing powder (salt, flour, or something similar). Or you can just skip right to the massage part. But please,

if at any time during the preparation of this trick, you feel like the plant is going to break, stop and find a more flexible plant.

This amazing feat was kindly donated to this book by my buddy Todd Karr.

PLANT MANAGER

What They See

You show the audience a branch from a bush or tree. It is dead and leafless. You lay the branch on the center of your spread out neckerchief. You roll the lifeless branch up in the center of your neckerchief and sprinkle a little water on it. When you open up the neckerchief the branch is covered with leaves—alive and thriving!

What You Need

✔ A square neckerchief or bandana
✔ 2 similar twigs about 10 inches long, covered with leaves
✔ A canteen or other water source (optional)

What You Do

Before you show the trick, pull off all the leaves from one of the twigs. Then lay the other twig (the one with leaves) on the ground (you can also place it on a table if there's one available). Lay the neckerchief over the leafy twig **1**. This is all secret preparation that you do prior to showing your friends the trick.

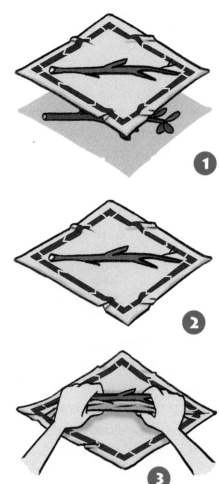

Now that you're ready to perform the trick, show your friends the leafless twig. Let them hold it if they wish. Lay it on the center of the neckerchief so that it's right over the hidden leafy twig **2**.

With both hands, grasp the visible twig and the hidden leafy twig through the neckerchief. Lift up all three items (the neckerchief and both twigs) and roll them up in the neckerchief **3**.

As you roll the neckerchief around its contents, keep your eye on the upper and lower corners of the neckerchief ❹. Just as the rolling-up process is complete, the top and bottom corners will switch places. That is, the corner that was closest to you will be farthest away, and vice-versa ❺. When that happens, stop rolling!

At this point sprinkle a little water on the neckerchief. Obviously, this doesn't do anything, but it does make an odd sort of sense that when you water the twig it will grow. If there's no water handy, or you're lost in the forest and water is scarce, you can skip this step.

To finish, grasp the upper and lower corners of the neckerchief and pull them apart ❻ revealing that the twig has apparently grown leaves! Pick the leafy twig up from the center of the neckerchief and let your friends check it out.

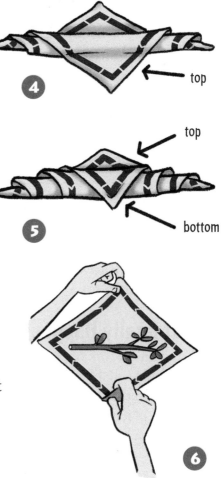

BE PREPARED

As they're curiously looking at the newly grown leaves, you casually pick up the neckerchief and the twig hidden under it and put them away in your pack. That way, if someone questions the neckerchief later you can remove it from your pack leaving behind the leafless twig. A good magician should always try to stay at least one step ahead of his audience!

This next one also uses a couple of twigs, but in a completely different way.

THE STICK STICKS

What They See

While on a cross-country hike you pick up a stick and ask, "Why do they call this a stick?" As an answer to your question, you hold the stick against your palm, where it magically and mysteriously clings as you say, "Because it sticks!"

What You Need

✔ Two nice, straight sticks about 10 inches long, at least one without any leaves

✔ A wristwatch (or a rubber band)

What Really Happens

Before you do this trick, you need to slip one of the sticks under your watchband ❶. This secret stick remains hidden throughout the trick. When you're ready, pick up the second stick and place it under the hidden stick ❷. Then, grip the visible stick in your left fingers ❸.

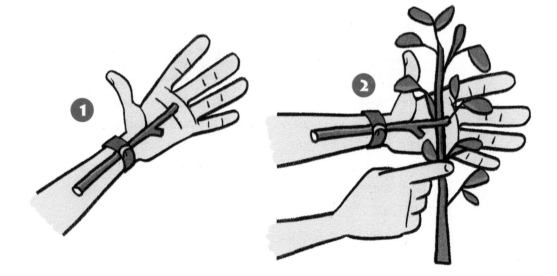

This is the point where you draw attention to yourself by holding up the stick with the back of your hand to the onlookers and asking the question, "Do you know why they call this a stick?" After you've listened to the answers people give to your question, you open your hand out flat ❹ as you say, "Because it sticks!"

You can shake your hand up and down a little and even tilt it palm down just as long as you keep the back of your hand toward the viewers and don't let them see the secret stick.

BE PREPARED

If you're not wearing a wristwatch, just slip the rubber band around your wrist and you're set. And just because I've described this with sticks doesn't mean you can't do this with silverware, pencils, chopsticks, straws, or any relatively straight objects of the right length.

Also, remember to listen and pay attention to the answers people give to your question. You never know when someone will say something funny that you can use in a future performance.

BURN, BABY, BURN

What They See

You're cooking around a campfire and suddenly you let out a little yelp of pain, "Ow!" Your concerned friends ask what happen and you respond, "I just burned myself on that pan." As you say this, you look at the tip of your thumb and there for all to see is a small red blister!

What You Need

✔ A key with a round hole in it ❶

What Really Happens

The key is in your pocket and never seen by the audience. When the time is right, put your hand into your pocket and press the hole of the key onto the tip of your thumb ❷. Hold it there and press hard for about 10 seconds. When you release pressure you will find that you've made a little raised circle on the tip of you thumb that looks exactly like a blister ❸. This will fade away pretty quickly, but you have 30 seconds or so to bring your hand out of your pocket and pretend to touch something hot. Try to act genuinely hurt. But do be careful not to actually touch anything hot; that's a stupid method for this trick. Give a small cry of pain loud enough so that your more sympathetic friends will ask you what happened. Show the injured thumb and pretend to be surprised that you burned yourself bad enough to raise an actual blister.

❶

And don't forget to continue to cook so that your pals realize that pain means nothing to you.

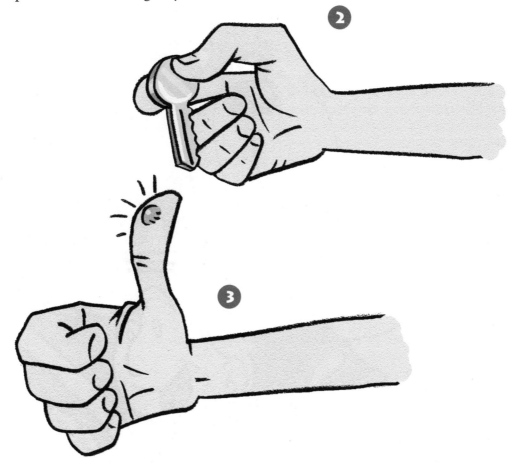

This great bit is the brainchild of my friend Jack Kent Tillar and it can be done anytime there's something really hot that you might conceivably touch by accident. I got a big reaction by apparently touching the baking pan when my mom was making cookies.

CHAPTER 3

CARD TRICKS

One thing you should always have in your pack when camping is a complete deck of cards. Every kid should know how to play some card games. Spades, Hearts, and Oh Hell are great for a small number of people, and Wink Murder is fantastic for a larger group sitting around a campfire. But you didn't buy this book to learn about card games did you? You want astounding, fry your friends' brains, over the top, spectacular card tricks. Don't worry, I've got 'em.

A SIMPLE (BUT DECEPTIVE) FORCE

To start things off I'll teach you what we magicians call "A Force." This allows you to offer a spectator a seemingly free choice of cards, but in reality they are "forced" to take the card you want them to choose. . . .

What They See

Your friend apparently cuts the deck anywhere he wishes and looks at the card he cut to. You know which card he cut to because you have cleverly controlled his actions and made him cut to the card you wish.

What You Need

✔ A deck of cards

What You Do

Before you begin you must secretly place the card you wish to force on top of the face-down deck **1**. The audience must not know that you know the identity of this top card.

When you're ready to start the trick, begin by asking your friend to hold out his left hand. Set the deck of cards face down into his outstretched palm. Ask him to cut off a portion of the deck and place it onto your upturned left palm, which you hold out for his convenience. He does so **2**.

With your right hand take the remaining cards from your friend's hand and place them cross-wise onto the cards in your left hand so that the two portions of the deck form an "X" **3**.

At this point you need to do a little bit of stalling so that the audience forgets which half of the deck is which. I usually point at the deck and say something along the lines of, "Now

you could've cut off any number of cards you wished. I didn't make you cut off 22 cards, or 30 cards, correct? You had a free choice?" He will agree.

With your right hand, lift up the upper portion of the cards and point at the top card of the remaining cards , as you say, "Take a look at the card you cut to." This is a bold lie. This is not the card they cut to; it's the original top card, but your little questions have distracted them enough to forget which half of the deck is which. This may seem daring, but trust me, it works every time.

When he takes a look at the card, caution him to remember it.

That's it. Congratulations! You've forced a card!

BE PREPARED

This force requires some sort of a surface on which to put the deck of cards. I've described it using your hands as that surface, but you can just as easily use a table or the floor. You just don't want the cards sliding around, or getting mixed up. If you're talking to another magician, it might be handy to know that us magicians call this force the "Cross Cut Force."

It's always a good idea when you have a card chosen to have the chooser show the card to the other audience members. This lets everyone feel more involved, and just in case the volunteer forgets which card he chose, he's got the audience's memory as backup. Plus, if the volunteer is the kind of person who would intentionally try to mess up your trick by fibbing about the identity of his card, the audience will know he's lying. Trust me, at some point in your magical career this will come in handy.

Keep in mind that this force is just a tool. It's not a trick. Now that you know how to force a card, you need some actual tricks with which to use it. We'll start with the simplest (but still effective)....

PREDICT-O-MATIC

What They See

Your friend cuts the deck. You remove your shoe and take out a folded piece of paper. When the paper is opened up it reads, "You will select the Eight of Clubs." Your friend looks at the card he cut to. It is the Eight of Clubs. Your friend realizes that you can predict the future. You promise to use your powers only for good.

What You Need

✔ A deck of cards.
✔ A prediction that states, "You will select the 8 of Clubs".
✔ A shoe (or some other place to hide the prediction)

What You Do

Before you present this trick there are a few preparations to take care of. Write the prediction. You can make this as simple as "8C" or as elaborate as "I have consulted the stray cat belonging to the sage who lives behind the dumpster at 7-11, and the all-knowing feline coughed up a furball in the shape of the Eight of Clubs. It is your destiny to choose that card. The stealthy one knows all." Whatever your prediction, fold it and put it in your shoe. Place the card mentioned in your prediction on top of the face-down deck. You're set to stun.

When you're ready to do this trick, follow the procedure outlined above in "A Simple (But Deceptive) Force," but when you instruct the person to "Take the card you cut to," you add, "but don't look at it yet, and don't let anyone else see it." Once they have the card in their hand you reassemble the deck and put it aside. Then show your hands empty and remove your shoe and say, "In my shoe I have prediction. I wrote this years ago about you. This is the only prediction I have." Remove the prediction, open it up, and have a friend read it aloud.

In your most dramatic voice you build up the trick by asking, "Could it be that my prediction is true? Is it possible that out of all the 52 cards you could have chosen, you selected the Eight of Clubs? Well there's one way to find out. Please turn your freely selected card around and show everybody. . . ."

Pause as your friend reveals the Eight of Clubs as you continue, saying triumphantly, "the Eight of Clubs!" while he shows the card to everyone.

BE PREPARED

Obviously you can predict the chosen card in an infinite number of ways. Try these. . . .

1

Secretly arrange a group of rocks on a bare patch of dirt in the shape of an 8 and a Club. Press them well down into the dirt so that they won't move if someone steps on them **1**. When you do this trick, position yourself so that in order to reach the cards to cut them your friend has to stand on these rocks. Have him chose a card and look at it (you secretly force the Eight of Clubs). Ask him if he feels like Mother Earth influenced his decision. When he says no, have him look under his feet. He might fall over.

Get some dishwashing liquid. Using a Q-tip (or your fingertip) write "8 of Clubs" on the inside of your left forearm in dishwasher liquid **2**. You can also write this prediction with the corner of a bar of soap dipped in water. When the soap

2

letters dry on your skin they will not be noticeable. Have the person chose a card (you secretly force the Eight of Clubs) and look at it and show it around to everyone–even you. Squat down and pick up a little bit of dusty, dry dirt in your right fingers. As you chant, "Eight of Clubs, Eight of Clubs, Eight of Clubs," Rub that dirt along the inside of your left forearm over the place where you wrote the prediction. The dirt will stick to the soap, revealing the writing in an eerie way 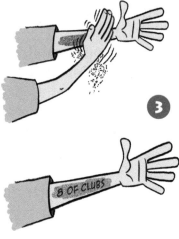. Very cool. At this point in your magical career I probably don't need to tell you that the soap writing is done in private before you show anyone this trick.

Arrange that your volunteer is someone whose cell phone number you know, and that he has that phone in his pocket. Before the trick, arrange seven cards on top of the deck so that they correspond to your volunteer's phone number. In other words, if you know that his phone number is 728-8265, you'd arrange the deck from the top down, a 7, a 2, an 8, an 8, a 2, a 6, and a 5 (the suits of the cards don't matter in this trick)

When you're ready to do the trick, ask your friend if he has a cell phone. If it's appropriate, act as if you don't even know whether he has a cell phone. Once he asserts that he does indeed have a phone, ask him to bring it out and hold it in his left hand. With his right have him cut off some cards from the top of the deck. Have him follow the forcing procedure up until the two halves of the deck are arranged in an "X" on your hand. At that point ask him if he felt like his phone influenced his choice in any way. Whatever he says, remove the top potion of the

X-ed cards and set them aside. Then spread over the top seven cards from the remaining portion of the deck. (These are the seven cards you set up before the trick.) Lift those seven cards up and hold them like a poker hand so that your friend can see the numbers of all seven cards  and ask him to read off the numbers in order. He'll say 7-2-8-8-2-6-5. If he doesn't react after saying the numbers, ask him to read them off again more slowly. Eventually it will dawn on him that somehow he has magically selected cards that match his phone number! This is a great trick, and a really freaky experience for your friend; the only drawback is that it doesn't work if there is a 1 or a 0 in your friend's number.

A couple of people have gone all out and actually hired a skywriter to skywrite the name of the chosen card overhead at the exact time they were forcing the card down on the ground. Pretty impressive. You'll probably need a rich uncle in order to do this one.

Next comes a rather unusual one…

KARATE CARD

What They See

You ask your volunteer to select a card and replace it into the deck. Your friends stare at you with a look of "What the heck?" as out of the blue you yell, "Hii Yaa!!!" and give the deck a fierce karate chop. You riffle up one end of the deck, and a card pops out about and inch. Turning the deck end-for-end, you riffle up the opposite end of the deck and out pops another card. Withdrawing the "popped-out" cards reveals that they are, in fact, two halves of a single card that has apparently been cut in half by your karate chop! When asked to name the card she chose, your friend says, "Seven of Spades." "Just as I thought," you say, as you turn over the two half-cards, revealing that the card that has been cut in half is the Seven of Spades!

What You Need

✔ A deck of cards.
✔ A duplicate Seven of Spades (from another deck with a matching back design) that you've torn through the middle

What You Do

Before the trick, you need to set up the deck. Place any card (except the Seven of Spades) face-down on to the table. On top of it place the two torn pieces of the Seven of Spades face-down. On top of that put the rest of the deck. And last, place the whole Seven of Spades on top of the deck (see ❷ for a diagram of this setup). The deck is set and so are you.

Carry out the course of action explained in "A Simple (but Deceptive) Force" to make sure that your friend selects the Seven of Spades. Don't worry about the torn card; it

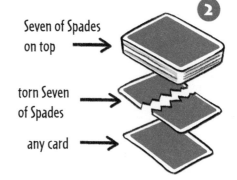

Seven of Spades
on top ➡

torn Seven
of Spades ➡

any card ➡

just goes along for the ride, and doesn't have any bearing on the actions of the force.

After your friend has looked at the selected Seven of Spades and shown it to everyone but you (remember, they shouldn't have any idea that you already know what the selected card is), have her replace it back onto the place from which she took it. You then drop the remainder of the deck on top of her selection. The scene is now like this: The Seven of Spades is somewhere near the center of the deck, and unbeknownst to the onlookers, two cards above it is the torn Seven of Spades].

With your right hand karate chop the deck across the middle as you let out a bloodcurdling yell.

Make a sort of fist with your left hand and place the deck under your left thumb. Make sure you have a nice tight grip, but that you're only holding the inner end of the deck–there should be no pressure on the outer three-quarters of the deck. Place your right thumb in the middle of the back of the deck and use your right fingers to bend up the outer end of the deck. (See ❸ to see what this grip looks like).

Let the cards rapidly flick off your right fingertips. The torn card should pop out a little bit from the end of the deck ❹.

Leave the card sticking out and rotate the deck and grip the opposite end in same left thumb grip you used before ❺. Flick through the end of the deck just like you did before. The other torn piece will pop out, leaving you with a half of a card sticking out of each end of the deck. Don't forget, at this point the audience doesn't know that they are pieces of a card, they think they are two different cards.

Set the deck, with the cards still sticking out, face down onto your friend's hand (or the ground or table) and then withdraw the two halves of card at the same time 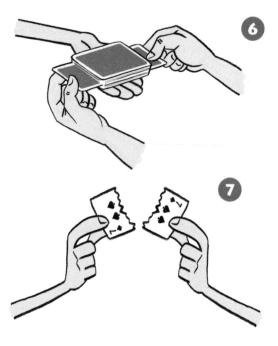. Make sure no one sees the faces of these two pieces of card.

Ask your friend to name the card she selected. After she says, "Seven of Spades," turn over the two pieces ⑦ to reveal you've successfully chopped her chosen card!

BE PREPARED

If you have trouble making the torn halves pop out when you flick through the deck, you can just spread through the deck until you get to the torn card. This is almost as good, but the pop out thing gives the trick a little extra "oomph."

You can also try this with the torn pieces face-up instead of face-down. This gives the trick a slightly different feel.

One of the things that makes this trick so effective is that to a "normal" person (as opposed to a magician) a deck that is missing even one card becomes useless. So cutting up a card (and thus "ruining" a deck) adds to the drama. This notion is also exploited in our next trick....

SEVEN AND THREE-QUARTERS

What They See

You spread out the deck of cards face-down and have your volunteer select one. He takes a look at it, shows it to the onlookers and then places it face-down onto the top of the deck. You give the deck a cut to lose his card somewhere in the center of the pack. Then placing the deck in your volunteer's hand, you concentrate, gazing off into the distance to gather your powers, and then bring your hand down dramatically onto the deck. "It is done," you say.

Taking it from your friend you spread through the face-down deck until you come to a face-up Two of Hearts. You cut the deck, bringing the face-up card to the top. Gazing at the Two of Hearts you calculate out loud, "Let's see, this is two, the wind is blowing at 4 miles per hour, there are two trees on our left and you have red hair. My computations tell me that your card now lies exactly 7 and three-quarters from the top." You continue, completely ignoring the befuddled expressions on your friends' faces, "Please hold out your hand."

Starting with the face-up Two of Hearts you deal cards one at a time from the top of the deck into the volunteer's hand, counting aloud, "One, two, three, four, five, six, seven." When you take the eighth card from the top of the deck it is seen to have a quarter torn off of it! As you deal it into the volunteer's hand you say, "And three-quarters." Waiting for the chuckles to subside you inquire, "And what was the name of the card you selected?" "Eight of Diamonds," you are told. After an appropriately dramatic pause, you turn over the next card revealing the Eight of Diamonds as you say, "The Eight of Diamonds, exactly seven and three-quarters down!"

What You Need

✔ A deck of cards.

✔ A card with the upper right corner torn off ❶. If you only have one deck and don't want to ruin it, use a Joker.

What You Do

There's a bit of a secret setup work to do before you can show this trick to anyone. Start by placing the torn card face-down onto the table (or ground, if you're actually preparing this at a campsite). Deal six cards face down onto the torn card, and then place any card face-up on of the pile of cards (in the above example it was the Two of Hearts, but the identity of this card doesn't matter). Drop the rest of the deck face-down on top. Check ❷ to make sure you've got this setup correct. Put the prepared deck in its box. You're ready to mystify.

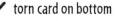

torn card on bottom

face-up card ❷

When you want to do this trick, take the deck out of the box making sure you don't leave any cards in the box. Set the box aside and spread the cards between your hands having your volunteer choose one. When you spread the cards for the selection, make sure you don't spread the bottom 15 cards or so, thus making certain that he doesn't pick one of the cards from your setup. As he's looking at his chosen card you square the deck up.

Ask him to show his card to everyone except you. Then have him place the selection on to the deck. Cut the deck, apparently losing the card somewhere in the center, but in reality what you've just done is covertly deposited your seven-card set up right on top of the selected card.

Hand the deck to the volunteer. Follow the description above where you dramatically bring your hand down onto the deck, saying "It is done," then take back the deck and spread it to reveal the face-up card. Cut the deck so that the face-up card is on top, which also secretly brings the rest of your setup cards to the top of the deck.

Next do the bit where you "calculate." This can be anything you wish; if you can tie it in with your actual surroundings and circumstances, so much the better. End your calculations by stating that the selected card lies "Seven and three-quarters from the top." People will look at you like you've lost your mind. Who ever heard of three-quarters of a card? Ignore their looks of pity, smile, and repeat yourself, "Your card lies seven and three-quarters from the top." Request that you friend hold out his hand so that you can deal cards into it.

Starting with the face-up card, deal cards one at a time from the top of the deck into the volunteer's hand, counting aloud, "One, two, three, four, five, six, seven..." Deal one card for each number you say. When you take the eighth card from the top of the deck it is seen to have a quarter torn off of it! As you deal it into the volunteer's hand  you say, "... and three-quarters." Wait 'til everyone is quiet and ask, "And what was the name of the card you selected?" Let's say he replies, "Eight of Diamonds," as in our example. Give 'em your best dramatic pause and then turn over the next card revealing the Eight of Diamonds  as you say, "The Eight of Diamonds, exactly seven and three-quarters down!"

BE PREPARED

As for tearing up a card, if you have two decks with matching back designs you don't have to use a joker for the torn card, you can just tear a card from the second deck and add it to the first. Then when this trick is over you put the torn card in your pocket leaving you with a complete deck for any other card trick you'd like to do.

In this trick the altered card is out in the open for all to see. But in the next one the audience is completely unaware on the existence of a modified card. It is based on a trick I first learned from a great old book called *The Royal Road to Card Magic* by Jean Hugard and Frederick Braue.

THIS I CANNOT FAIL TO DO

What They See

Your audience is sure you've made a massive mistake, and believing that there is absolutely no way for you to bring about a successful conclusion to your trick, they are even more taken in when you emerge triumphant in the end.

What You Need

✔ A deck of cards.
✔ A pair of scissors.
✔ A table or some other flat surface (the floor works just fine).
✔ An audience of at least one person.

What You Do

Prior to showing the trick, cut off about 1/8 of an inch from the end of one of the cards. Round off the corners of the cut end so that they look close to the way the other corners look ❶. This is known in the business as a "short card." Place the short card on top of the face-down deck. Obviously, this secret preparation happens when you're by yourself, before you present the trick.

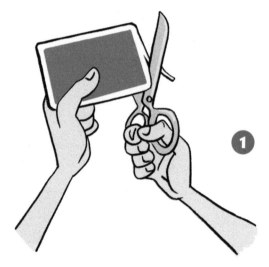

When you are ready, ask someone to help you. Spread the deck out between your hands in the standard "Pick a Card" gesture. The clichéd phrase that magicians utter at this point is, "Pick a card, any card." If that fits your personality, by all means say it, but if that doesn't seem like something that you'd say, then say something different. You can say, "Reach in and grab one," or "Kindly select a card," whatever seems the most like you. When he's made his selection, ask him to show it around to everyone else. Caution him not to let you see the card. As he's looking at the card, you square the deck and place it on the table. The short card is still on top.

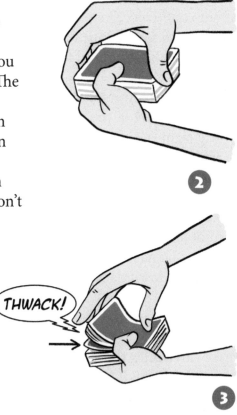

After he's looked at the card and shown it around have him replace it face-down on top of the deck. Have him give the deck a complete cut, apparently losing his card in the center of the deck. Even though you don't know what his selected card is, you do know that it is directly above the short card. Keep this valuable bit of knowledge to yourself.

Pick up the deck and hold it with both hands as in ❷. Use your right fingers to bend up the outer end of the deck. Let the cards slowly flick off your right fingertips. The cards will make a sort of whirring noise. When you reach the short card the whirring noise will be interrupted by a slightly louder "thwack!" Stop right there—don't let any more cards flick off your right fingertips ❸. Relax your right hand's grip so that the cards unbend, but keep the two halves of the deck separate. Your right hand places its cards onto the table and then comes back and grasps the left hand's cards and places them onto the cards on the table. To the spectators it looks like you simply cut the cards, but in reality you have positioned the short card on top of the deck and secretly controlled the selected card to the bottom of the deck!

Ask the participant to cut off about 1/3 of the deck and place the cut-off section to the right of the deck. Point to where you want him to place his portion ❹. Before he cuts the deck, grasp his arm dramatically and instruct him, "This is all about confidence. As you cut the cards, you have to say in your most confident voice, 'This I cannot fail to do.'" He does so.

Next, have him cut off about ½ of the remaining part of the deck and place it to the right of the other two piles. Once again, point to where you wish him to put the cards ❺. And again, as he is reaching to cut the deck, grasp his arm and command him, "Again, as you cut the cards, you must say in your most confident voice, 'This I cannot fail to do.'"

Once he has followed your instructions there will be three face-down packets on the table, and unknown to the audience the selected card will be on the bottom of the left-hand packet. Announce to everyone, "If you had the proper confidence as you cut the cards, one of the bottom cards of these three piles should be the card you selected. My job is to determine which one. I'm going to turn over each pile and I'll say, 'I think this is your card,' if I think it's your card. And I'll say, 'I don't think this is your card,' if I don't think it's your card. If I'm right, please don't anybody say anything. If I'm wrong, please don't say anything. In other words, don't say anything—keep a poker face."

With your left hand, pick up the pile furthest to the right. You need to use a specific grip here, because in a minute you're going to do a tricky move, and you want your actions when you're doing the tricky move to be identical to when you're not doing anything sneaky. Your four fingers grip one long side of the cards and your thumb is on the opposite side. About half of the packet is concealed by your left fingers and palm. This is pretty important, so take a look at ❻ to make sure you've got it right.

Turn your left hand palm up to show everyone the card at the face of the packet. Announce the name of the card there and then say, "I don't believe this is your card." Turn your left hand palm down as you caution the audience, "Remember, please don't indicate if I'm right or wrong." With your right hand reach under the left hand's packet and withdraw the bottom card and set it aside face down onto the table off to the right.

Drop the remainder of the left hand's cards on to the right hand pile of the two piles still on the table. Pick up this combined pile in your left hand in exactly the same grip you used for the first pile. Turn your left hand palm up to show everyone the card on its face. Announce the card and say again, "I don't believe this is your card." Turn your left hand palm down as you remind everyone, "Make sure you make no sign whether I'm right or wrong." Again withdraw the bottom card of the left-hand's packet and place it face-down with the first card off to the right.

Drop the left hand's cards onto the one remaining pile and pick up this combined pile using the same left hand grip as before. Turn the deck face up and announce the name of the card exhibited on its face. This is the selected card, but you don't let on that you know that. Keep your face and your attitude exactly as they were on the first two cards and say, "Hmm, I don't think this is your card either."

Turn your left hand down and carry out the following secret move: Reach under the face-down deck with your palm-up right hand. Your right middle finger touches the bottom card of the deck and secretly pushes it to the left a little less than an inch, so that it sticks out the back of the deck. The back of the left hand conceals the protruding card. shows what this looks like from underneath. In a continuing action the right middle finger moves slightly to

57

the right contacting the card second from the bottom of the deck and pulls it out from under the deck and places it off to the right with the other two cards there. Everyone thinks this is the selected card, but the selected card is still on the bottom of the deck in the left hand. Make sure the bottom card—the selection—is still in place protruding from the left end of the deck.

Say to your participant, "Well that usually works, but on the rare times when it fails there is a sure-fire method for finding the card. Please name a number from five to ten." Let's say they say six. With your right hand reach under the face-down deck and withdraw the card second from the bottom. This is easy because the bottom card is still pushed back from the front edge of the deck. Place this card face-up onto the table, counting "One."

Again reach under the face-down deck and take the card second from the bottom and pull it out and turn it face-up on the table counting "Two." Repeat this counting action until you get to the chosen number, in this case, six. On the chosen number reach a bit further under the deck and withdraw the actual bottom card. This is the selection, so keep it face-down so no one can see it; remember, they think the selected card is one of the three face-down cards off to the right. Announce, "I now hold in my hand your selected card."

The audience will be so happy because they think you've really messed up. Nevertheless, you continue by asking, "Please, for the first time, name the card you selected." The spectator names the card you're holding. Pretend to be a bit confused as you sneakily glance at the card face-down on the table that they believe to be the selection as you repeat the name of the card as if to make sure you heard them right.

Pause dramatically, smile and say, "And here it is, your card!" as you triumphantly turn over the card in your hand. Rest assured everyone will dive at the card on the table that they thought was the selected card.

BE PREPARED

You'll notice I've given you more specific dialogue you need to say for this trick than I have for some of the others. It's also difficult because there are a lot more things going on here. It's really critical that no one says anything when you're turning up the three piles and announcing that none of them is the selected card. You don't necessarily have to use the words I give you here (in fact it's probably better if you use words that sound more like you), but it is important that you make everyone aware of what you expect.

This is the toughest of all the card tricks in this book, and not just because it involves the most sleight-of-hand. It's also because it requires the most acting to pull off. In order to get the most out of this, you really need to be able to nudge people into convincing themselves that you have hopelessly screwed up, and that there's no way for you to get out of the hole you've put yourself in. So, if you put in the practice needed to make it smooth and are a good actor, then I predict this will quickly become your favorite card trick. It not only really fools people, but it really engages them emotionally. They feel like they have caught you in a huge error, and there is absolutely no way for you to rescue yourself. This is really like a thrilling roller-coaster ride for the audience. Not bad for a card trick.

CHAPTER 4
MAGIC OF THE MIND

Magicians who do mindreading and psychic stunts are called "mentalists." They call their tricks "mentalism." These next few tricks range from creepy to comic, but they all involve supposed mystic powers. If you own a turban, put it on now.

EXTRA SENSORY DECEPTION

What They See

You're sitting around a campfire with your scouting buddies and the talk turns to merit badges. You casually mention that you have recently earned a merit badge in mindreading. When your pals are through scoffing at you, you offer to demonstrate what you had to do to meet the requirements of the Mindreading Merit Badge.

Taking out a pad of paper, you ask people to call out merit badge subjects. As people name merit badges, you write each one down on a separate piece of paper and wad each paper up and drop it into an upturned cap. When you've filled up the cap, or you have about a dozen paper wads, whichever comes first, have somebody mix up the papers in the cap and choose one. Caution him to keep the paper hidden tightly in his hand. The remainder of the papers are dumped into the campfire.

Gazing trance-like into the smoke of the burning papers, your eyes roll back into your head. Suddenly you awake and announce, "I've got it." Taking the pad of paper you quickly jot down something, and fold up the sheet with the writing inside. "I have taken a supernatural journey and had a psychic vision. On this sheet of paper I have written down the name of one merit badge.

"For the first time," you continue, "please open the paper and read out to everyone the name of the merit badge you've chosen." He does so. Let's suppose he says, "Archeology."

"Interesting," you state, as you unfold the paper you're holding and turn it around so that everyone can read that you've written, "ARCHEOLOGY."

What You Need

✔ A pad of paper
✔ A pencil
✔ A campfire
✔ A hat
✔ A merit badge in mindreading (optional)

What You Do

When you're ready to do this trick, bring out the pad of paper. Explain that you're going to write down a whole bunch of merit badge names. Ask people to suggest various merit badges.

Let's say the first badge called out is Archeology. You repeat out loud, "Archeology," write ARCHEOLOGY on the

top sheet of the pad, tear the sheet from the pad, wad it up, and drop it in the hat. Keep the pad tilted up so that no one can see what you're writing.

Let's say the second badge named is Basketry. You repeat out loud, "Basketry," but write ARCHEOLOGY on the next sheet of the pad, tear the sheet from the pad, wad it up, and drop it in the hat. Again, keep the pad tilted up so that no one can see what you're writing.

Let's say the third badge called is Bird Study. You say, "Bird Study," but secretly write ARCHEOLOGY on the next sheet, tear it off, wad it up, and drop it into the hat.

Let's say the next badge called is Bugling. You say, "Bugling," write ARCHEOLOGY, tear it off, wad it up, and drop it into the hat.

That's right, no matter what badge is called out, you secretly write the same thing on every piece of paper. Of course it's critically important that you keep your pad tilted up so no one sees what you write. They must be convinced that each time you write down the named merit badge. You can encourage that conviction by doing subtle little things. For instance, if someone says Architecture, you ask, "Is that spelled A-R-C-I, or A-R-C-H-I?" Or you can start to write the badge that was actually named, but intentionally misspell it. So you tear that page off the pad, toss the page with the misspelled word aside so that people get a glimpse of it, saying, "Oops, that's not how you spell "Entrepreneurship."

When you've got a capful of duplicate wads of paper, say, "Okay, that's enough to give us a good range." Then have someone mix up the paper wads in the cap and select one. Ask him to hold his selection tightly in his clenched fist so that no one can see it. Have someone toss the remaining paper wads into the campfire, thus destroying the evidence. Fire is your friend!

Stare into the smoke and pretend to go into your spirit trance. Awaken from your journey with a start, write down the prediction—in this case ARCHEOLOGY—and fold up the paper with the writing inside.

Say the bit about taking a supernatural journey blah, blah, blah, and have the person open up his chosen paper wad and read out the chosen merit badge. He'll say "Archeology" (or whatever the first badge was).

You say, "Interesting," and then unfold the paper you're holding so that only you can see what's written there. Pause for dramatic effect, and turn the paper to reveal that your prediction reads, "ARCHEOLOGY."

BE PREPARED

There are currently over 120 merit badges available to the Boy Scout. If you're doing a more formal show you should try to keep people on track and not allow things to slow down by letting people discuss whether something someone nominates as a merit badge is in fact legit. On the other hand, if it's just you and some pals sitting around, a spirited debate does no harm, and probably adds appeal to the proceedings.

Of course, this trick doesn't have to be done with merit badges. It can be done with anything: celebrities, fruits and vegetables, baseball players, geometric shapes, anything.

Also, you can do this without a campfire. You just don't want people opening up the unchosen paperwads (or they'll take away your mindreading merit badge). I've found the best thing is to just toss them aside as if they're completely unimportant. If you don't attach any value to them, then chances are the audience won't either.

Here's another trick that uses pretty much the same props, but it's a tad more creepy. Which is a good thing.

DEAD OR ALIVE

What They See

The all-seeing mentalist tears a sheet of paper into nine squares. Passing them out to people, he asks that each person write down the name of a famous living person. However, one person is singled out and asked instead to write the name of a famous dead person. Have the papers collected in a cap and mixed up. The cap is held high so that you can't see into it, but still you're able to reach in and pick out the dead person's name. You state that it was colder than the living names!

What You Need

✔ A piece of notebook or computer paper
✔ A few pencils or pens (you can get by with one, but it saves a bunch of time if all nine folks have their own)
✔ A cap
✔ Nine spectators

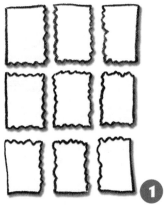

What Really Happens

This is exceptionally simple. When you tear a piece of paper into nine pieces, you'll see that all of the pieces have at least one smooth, straight edge except the center piece. It's the only one with four torn edges ❶. We'll call this piece the "key piece."

When you hand out the pieces make sure you notice who gets the key piece. That's the person you instruct to write the dead celebrity's name.

Have all the pieces gathered up in a cap and mixed up. Have the person hold the cap up so that you can't see inside it ❷. State that because the dead person's name has a completely different energy, your sensitive fingertips will be able to pick it out from among the living names.

All you have to do is find the key piece. The easiest way to do this is to sort of scoop all the pieces into a small pile on one side of the inside of the hat. Then pick them up one at a time (keep the piece inside the hat out of view—you don't want the audience to think you can see the papers) and feel around each edge. If you feel a smooth edge, discard that piece to the other side of the hat.

When you find the key piece, start acting. Let your eyes roll back into your head. Pretend like a sudden chill has startled you. Say, "I sense the icy presence of the lifeless. This must be the dead celebrity." Bring forth the piece of paper and slump down as if you've gone through a terrible ordeal.

Please don't let the simplicity of the method keep you from doing this. This trick will fool people.

BE PREPARED

If the idea of using a dead person's name is too eerie for you, you can use eight boy's names and one girl's, or eight vegetables and one fruit, whatever you wish.

If you don't have a cap, you can use a paper bag or a large bowl. It's even possible to do this by having them mix up the pieces and place them in your hands behind your back or under a table.

And if you don't have nine participants, you can do this with as few as two. Simply have one person write all eight of the living names and one person write the dead name. Of course you make sure to hand the key piece of paper to the dead name writer.

One of the ways that people invent tricks is to combine two old tricks to make one new trick. A cool thing to do is to combine this trick with "Burn, Baby, Burn". Instead of saying that the dead person's name is colder than all the others, you state that the dead name is actually much hotter than the living names. After you withdraw the paper with dead person's name and show it, you touch the name with your fingertip and let out a blood-curdling scream and drop the slip of paper. Say that the name actually burned you, and show everyone the blister on your fingertip as evidence. Using the method explained in the Blister trick, you make the blister while people are writing the nine names. This makes this trick extra creepy.

Sometimes it's fun to leave people feeling creepy, but if you want to lighten the mood a bit, try this next quickie.

NO JOKE

What They See

You invite someone to help you in a game of brain to brain communication. Explain that you are going to attempt to send a thought from your brain into his. Showing the audience a piece of cardboard, the magician questions the helper, "I've written a single word on the other side of this card. Do you have any idea what that word is?"

The volunteer responds, "No."

The magician says, "Correct!" as he swivels the card around to show everyone that printed there in large letters is the word "NO."

The audience laughs to show its appreciation for your wit.

What You Need

✔ A piece of cardboard with the word NO printed on it

What Really Happens

Just follow along with the description in "What They See." Just make sure you play it seriously up until you reveal the word "NO." The more you build this up like it's going to be a great mystery, the greater the audience's laughter.

BE PREPARED

The card should be of the proper size for the audience you're performing for. If it's just you and your pal, you can use a small piece of paper or an index card. If you're doing a show in someone's den then a piece of notebook or computer paper is good. If you're performing at the halftime show of the Superbowl you'll probably want something a bit larger.

Whatever size paper you use, you'll want to make sure that the writing doesn't bleed through so that it can't be seen before you want it to.

If you enjoy this bit and find that you have a knack for the humorous, here's a more elaborate, and more ridiculous, sample of comedy mentalism. . . .

TELEPATHY FOR TWO

What They See

Explaining to the audience that you are going to turn one of them into a mindreader, you select a person and apparently hypnotize him. As you blindfold him with a neckerchief so that he cannot see, you say in your most pompous voice, "He is now in a complete hypnotic trance and therefore able to take advantage of his psychic powers which have heretofore lied dormant."

You then hand the new mindreader a cooking pot lid and a spoon. Address someone in the audience, "Please hold up any number of fingers from one to ten. Our psychic will receive that number and strike the ancient and sacred gong (you point to the pot lid) precisely that many times.

Let's say that the person holds up six fingers. "Have you received the number?" you ask the assistant.

He responds in his best sleepy-creepy voice, "Yeees."

"All right, strike the gong," you direct him.

He begins to hit the gong in a slow rhythm. Once. Twice. Three. Four. Five. Six. Just as he is about to bring his hand down to strike the gong for the seventh time, you grab his arm and say, "Correct! Six was the number! Amazing ladies and gentlemen!"

You continue talking to the audience, "Now if you'll each hold up some object. Something simple that you have on your person or in your pocket, perhaps the great swami will be able to use his amazing powers to identify it.

Pointing to someone's watch you say, "What is this? Take your time with this one." He responds, "A watch."

Hold up a pair of glasses, saying, "You should be able to see clearly through this one."

He responds, "Glasses."

You touch someone's ear and ask, "What's this, can you hear me?"

He says, "An ear."

Touch his hair, "And this? Can you hair me?"

He says, "His hair."

Touch his nose, "Everyone knows this."

"His nose."

"One final test for the great one." Taking a coin from the spectator, you hold it up and say, "Spend your time. Think. What is this?"

He says, "Money."

"Okay, coin-centrate. What kind of money?"

He says, "It's a coin."

"What denomination is the coin?" you ask.

He responds, "Presbyterian."

You ask again, "Very funny. I'll give you ten seconds to tell us the value of the coin."

"Oh," he says, "a dime."

You reply, "Very good, now please, without any hints, tell us the date."

He declares, "The date? Oh that's easy, it's Saturday, May 23, 2009!" as he states that day's date.

"That's correct! Today is in fact May 23, 2009! Ladies and gentlemen, let's have a big hand for the world's most mental mindreader!" He removes the blindfold and bows to laughter and applause.

What You Need

✔ A pal willing to rehearse for a few minutes

✔ A decent sized audience (I'd say a minimum of five people)

What Really Happens

Basically you just follow the script as outlined above. You'll almost always be able to spot someone wearing glasses and a watch. It's best to have a coin in your pocket just in case no one holds up money. You can sneak the coin from your pocket in your closed hand and then bend over one of the audience members and then stand straight up holding the coin, saying "One final test for the great one. . . ." They'll think you borrowed the coin from the audience member. Go on with the trick as usual, then at the end while everyone is laughing you simply put the coin back in your pocket.

Because you're doing most of the talking and most of the action depends on you, you can get someone to be the assistant almost on the spur of the moment. Just a few minutes' run-through will teach them everything they need to know to get loads of laughs.

BE PREPARED

Here are a few more bits you can throw in if you spot the right objects.

If someone holds up a knife, "Look sharp, you can cut it."

If someone holds up a compass, "Orient yourself and name this one."

If you spot any red item, "Name the color of this item. Red-y? Go."

This is obviously more like a skit or play than an actual magic trick, but once you have the reputation for being a magician, your friends will love you in this role. When I do this, I try to play it as serious as I can. That seriousness, contrasted with the silliness of the actual situation seems to make this even funnier. This next one is, to me, the funniest of them all. . . .

FEET OF FORTUNE

What They See

You explain to a friend that you can predict his future by reading the psychic vibes given off by his shoe. He removes his shoe and hands it to you. You stare intently at it, saying, "You will soon be embarking on a short journey." You pause for a moment to allow him to contemplate just what this excursion might be, and then you toss his shoe as far as you can.

Your prediction has come true. He embarks on a short journey—to retrieve his shoe!

What You Need

A friend with a shoe (go for someone who won't beat you up at the end of this joke)

What Really Happens

You say, "For my next experiment I shall employ the ancient and almost forgotten art of shoe reading." Addressing your most understanding pal, request that he give you his shoe. Hold it in your hand and stare intently at it as if you're receiving mystical sensations. If you're the kind of person who's not above sticking his nose into the shoe and taking a big whiff in order to generate a laugh, now is the time to indulge that impulse.

When you've milked the situation for all the audience will bear, say, "I have received all truth the shoe can impart. Your distant future seems cloudy, I can't get any reading on what the far-off future has in store for you. But I did get a definite vibe on the near future. Your shoe did convey to me that in the very near future you will be going on a short journey." Pause a moment to allow your friend to contemplate what marvelous journey he may be undertaking, and then fling the shoe as far as circumstances allow. There may be a brief look of puzzlement on your friend's face, but it will quickly dawn on him that your prophecy is correct!

BE PREPARED

This is a funny practical joke. As with all practical jokes it's very important that you not display any nastiness or cruelty. Everyone involved, those watching as well as those participating, should know that this is all in fun and that you'd be laughing just as loud had the gag been played on you.

That said, you still might want to pick someone for this who you can outrun.

CHAPTER 5

GEAR UP

If you're a scout who does magic, people will expect
you to do tricks with scouting stuff. The tricks
detailed in this section enable you to more than
satisfy those demands.

(UN)TRUE NORTH

What They See

All scouts have a compass, whether it's hooked to their belt, imbedded in the handle of their knife, or part of their glow-in-the-dark decoder ring. So you should have no trouble when you ask to borrow a compass. Place the borrowed compass on a table as everyone sits around it.

Say, "As everyone knows, a compass always indicates north. I'd like to try a small psychic experiment today. I'd like to see if we can make the needle of the compass move with our minds. Everyone focus your attention on the needle of the compass. Concentrate. I am going to count backwards from ten to one. As I do so I want you all to focus as intently as you can." You begin counting, "Ten. Nine. Focus on the needle. Eight. Seven. Six. All your energy on the needle. Five. Four. We're going to try to make the needle move on 'One.' Three. Two. Focus. One!" The instant you say "One," the needle of the compass jumps and spins out of control!

What You Need

- ✔ A compass
- ✔ A table and chair(s)
- ✔ A strong magnet
- ✔ Tape
- ✔ Long pants (or shorts that come down to your knees)
- ✔ That's right, to control a compass with your brain, you don't even need a brain!

What Really Happens

The needle of a compass is actually a small magnet that is attracted to a magnetic field at the northern end of the earth. Since the force of earth's magnetic field is pretty weak, all you have to do to get the compass needle to move as if by magic is place a stronger magnet near the compass.

Of course, the tricky part is to do that without it being obvious what you're doing.

In a private place, tape the magnet to the front of your leg, just above the knee. Pull down your pants leg to hide the magnet You're ready to amaze.

When you wish to perform this trick, sit in a chair at the table. Gather all the onlookers around a table. If there are other chairs available, have people sit down, but if yours is the only chair, have them stand as close to the table as possible. The idea is to make sure that no one is able to see under the table where all the dirty work takes place.

If you can borrow a compass, do so. By borrowing it you are emphasizing that the compass is free from trickery. If no other compass is available, bring yours out. Place the compass on the table over the spot where the magnet stuck to your leg lies out of sight under the table 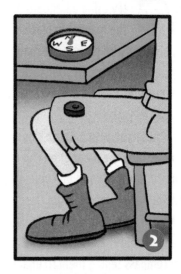. Make sure that the compass is far enough away from the hidden magnet that it is not yet affected by it.

Have people try touching the compass and blowing on it to convince themselves that it is not influenced by any outside forces.

All that remains is for you to repeat the story about moving the compass needle by group concentration. Counting backward from ten to one helps to build the suspense and to dramatize the moment when the needle moves, so lay it on thick. When you get down to "One" in the count simply move your knee up under the table so that it comes near the compass 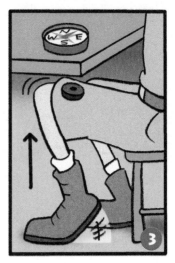. The needle will jump spectacularly. Immediately move your knee back down so that the compass returns to normal. At the same time, in your best fake

compass above knee

psychic imitation, slump back in your chair as if you are exhausted and the strain of your intense concentration has sapped all your strength.

BE PREPARED

 If you find yourself without tape, try using a bandaid or two to hold the magnet in place. You can also experiment with placing the magnet in the toe of your shoe or inside your sock and secretly moving your foot up toward the tabletop instead of your knee.

You can also accomplish this effect without a table. Tape the magnet on the underside of your forearm ❹ and pull your sleeve down to hide it. Have someone hold the compass in his palm and have everyone crowd around. Have them all hold their hands above and around the compass telling them to imagine their psychic energy flowing from their fingertips.

Your hands are there with the onlookers ❺. Make sure you keep the magnet far enough from the compass that you don't make it jump too soon. Do the same counting backwards from ten to one speech, and as you say "One" thrust your hands forward a few inches thus causing the compass to jump. While this variation is still startling, I don't think it's quite as good as the technique using your knee because in that method all the secret movement is hidden out of sight under the table.

Here's one that's a little less freaky and a lot funnier.

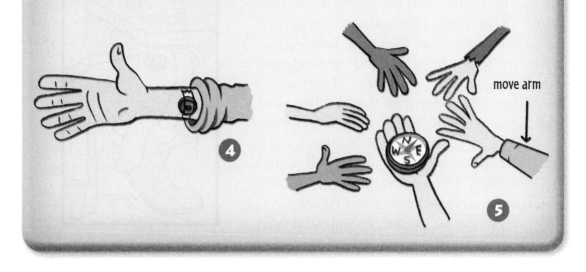

move arm

WATER ON THE BRAIN

What They See

You ask one of your den-mates to remove his cap, show everyone that it's empty, and have him hold it above his head upside down, with the opening on top. Next, you exhibit a small paper cup in your left hand and a water filled canteen in your right hand. At this point you appear confused as to what you should do next. As you say, "The cup goes in the hat—no wait the cup doesn't go in the hat," you place the cup into the hat and then remove it.

"Oh yes," you continue, "The water goes in the hat." You pour water right into your friend's hat.

"Oh wait, that's not right," you say, your confusion and incompetence becoming more evident. As he realizes that you have just poured water directly into his hat, your friend's expression will change from one of pleasure to one of pain. You look at his hat and then sheepishly at the cup still in your left hand.

"Oh! I believe I was supposed to put the cup in the hat before I poured the water in. Yes, I was definitely supposed to put the cup in first."

With a hopeful look you say, "I believe I have a solution." You lower the cup into the hat for an instant. When you bring it out of the hat the cup is full of water, which you pour back into the canteen. Then you triumphantly grasp the hat and show your audience that it is not only empty, but also completely dry!

What You Need

✔ A canteen, glass or bottle of water
✔ Two small paper cups which you'll combine into one
    "tricky cup"
✔ A pair of scissors
✔ A pal with a hat

What You Do

The first step is to prepare your "tricky cup." Cut out the bottom from one of the cups. Cut off the top rim of the other cup ❶. If you nest the bottomless cup inside the rimless cup it will look like one regular cup.

Place the tricky cup and the canteen of water where you can get to them easily and you're all set.

Get a friend who's wearing a cap to stand up in front of your audience. Have him remove his cap, show it empty, and hold it above his head upside down ❷. Caution him that no matter what happens he should not remove the cap from atop his head.

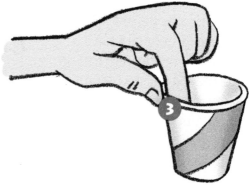

Now you follow along with the "What They See" description: You hold the tricky cup in your left hand with your fingers on the inside of the cup ❸ and an open canteen in your right hand. Act confused as to what you should do next. Say, "The cup goes in the hat." As you place the cup into the hat, your fingers and thumb separate the two parts of the tricky cup, secretly leaving the outside, rimless cup in the hat ❹. Remove the bottomless cup as you say, "No, wait, the cup doesn't go in the hat." Make sure your left hand holds the cup so that no one can see that it doesn't have a bottom.

"Oh yes," you continue, "The water goes in the hat." Pour water right into your friend's hat, being careful to make sure that the water goes into the rimless cup that you secretly loaded there. Pour in enough water to fill the rimless cup just over half full. Remind the volunteer not to move the hat; you don't want the cup to tip over at this point!

"Oh wait, that's not right," you say, acting even more confused. Look at his hat and then at the cup still in your left hand. "Oh! I believe I was supposed to put the cup in the hat before I poured the water in. Yes, I was definitely supposed to put the cup in first." Pause long enough to let the situation sink in to your audience. You want everyone to realize that this guy is holding a hatful of water.

Say, "I believe I have a solution." Slowly lower the bottomless cup into the hat, secretly lowering it right into the rimless cup of water . Inside the hat, nest the cups together as one and bring them out together full of water. Pour the water from the cup back into the canteen. Proudly turn the hat toward your audience, showing them that it is empty and dry. Everything worked out just fine!

BE PREPARED

If the person holding the hat is as tall or taller than you, you might have a hard time reaching up to pour the water into the hat. If that's the case, you can have him sit in a chair or have him hold the hat out in front of himself at eye level. Anything is okay so long as the person can't see into the hat.

Next up is a much more elaborate, and to my mind, even more hilarious take on the "spectator's cap in trouble" theme.

CAP-CAKE

What They See

After enjoying a fine meal around the campfire our hero conjures up dessert. Flour, milk, and egg dumped into someone's cap are magically cooked and transformed into a cupcake—a real cupcake you can actually eat!

What You Need

✔ A two-pound paper bag of flour like they sell in the grocery
✔ A raw egg
✔ A pushpin
✔ A toothpick
✔ A bowl
✔ Access to a water faucet and sink
✔ A cupcake (either without frosting or with hard frosting)
✔ A spectator with a cap (if he has red hair, so much the better)
✔ One of those little plastic coffee creamers
✔ Glue

What Really Happens

Since not one of the items used in this trick is really what it seems, there's quite a bit of pre-trick preparation for this one, so we'll take it in steps. . . .

Step One—The Bag of Flour

Open the top of the paper bag of flour. You want to do this carefully by undoing the glue places so that there are no tears in the bag.  shows you what it looks like fully opened. Dump all the flour into something else (a big Ziploc bag is good for this).

Drop a pinch of flour back into the bag and fold the top closed. Shake up the bag to coat the inside of the bag with a light dusting of flour. Open the bag and dump out any remaining flour.

Put the cupcake down into the bottom of the empty flour bag. Lay the flour bag down on its back so that the label where it says "FLOUR" is facing up. Fold the top of the bag down three times ❷. Unfold the folds you just made and put a pinch of flour into the first fold ❸, and then again fold the top of the bag down three times with the flour inside. Give the rest of the flour to your mom and ask her to make you some bread.

Step Two—The Egg

You're going to create what magicians call a "blown egg." That's an empty eggshell without any yolk or egg white inside. To accomplish this seemingly impossible feat you need the egg, the bowl, the pushpin, and the toothpick. Holding the egg over the bowl (in case there's an accident), make a small hole in the narrow end of the egg with the pushpin ❹. Still using the pushpin, make another hole in the other end of the egg. Use the pushpin to chip away at the edges of this hole to make it slightly larger ❺. Push the toothpick into this larger hole and swirl it around to break up the yolk inside the shell.

Holding the egg over the bowl, blow into the smaller hole so that the insides of the egg squirt out the larger hole into the bowl ❻. It may take a few puffs to get everything out. If you're having trouble, make the holes in the egg a little bigger.

Once the shell is basically empty, hold it under a water faucet with the larger hole facing up. When the egg is about one-quarter full of water, withdraw it from under the water stream. Shake the egg to rinse the inside. Don't forget to cover the holes with your fingers while you're shaking, so the water doesn't go everywhere! Blow the water out of the egg into the sink. Repeat this rinsing of the inside of the eggshell a couple of times until the water runs clear. Give the bowl of egg insides to your

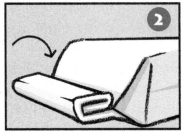

mom and tell her to use it in the bread she's making. Set the empty eggshell aside to dry.

Step Three—The Creamer

Peel back the foil top of the coffee creamer just enough 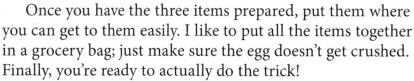 so that you can empty the white fluid out into the sink (please don't let your mom put this stuff in the bread). Use water to rinse it out. Dry it off and fold the top back and press it flat so that the creamer looks like it hasn't been opened. If you can't get the top to lay flat use a little glue to hold it closed.

Once you have the three items prepared, put them where you can get to them easily. I like to put all the items together in a grocery bag; just make sure the egg doesn't get crushed. Finally, you're ready to actually do the trick!

This can be done as part of a longer show, but I think it's even more fun to do it after everyone has had their dinner and are sitting comfortably around the campfire. Ask someone with a cap if they'd care for a little dessert. Regardless of their reply ask them to stand up in front of the group.

Say, "The first thing we need to make a delicious pastry is a nice baking pan. Who has a baking pan I can borrow? I promise you'll get it back." You'll be met with blank stares (especially if you are, in fact, outside around a campfire). "No one?" You continue, addressing your standing volunteer, "That's okay, we'll use your cap. Please remove it and let's make sure it's nice and clean." Show the inside of the cap around to everyone. You want to make sure that they all know you began with an empty hat. Ask him to hold the cap above his head with both hands . If the cap is the kind with an adjustable strap in the back, adjust his grip so the strap is toward the back, away from the audience; you don't want the audience to be able to see through the little half moon cutout.

Grab your bag of props and pull forth the bag of flour. Say, "I have here about one pound of flour, but for our demonstration we only need a few teaspoons." As you unfold the top of the bag, try to get as much of the bit of flour you deposited there into your fingers. Any flour that falls to the ground only adds to the illusion that the bag is full of flour. Dunk the hand with the flour in it partway down into the bag and apparently grab a pinch of flour. (Don't go all the way to the bottom, the bag is supposed to be half full.) Bring out your hand and apparently drop the pinch of flour into the cap, trying to get as much flour into the air as possible to make a little flour "cloud" above the cap.

Reach back down into the bag and apparently get another pinch of flour. Bring your hand out and pretend to put the second pinch of flour into the cap. Start to reach back into the bag a third time, but stop and say, "This is gonna take forever, let's just use it all."

Making sure that the top of the flour bag is well below the top edge of the cap, seemingly dump all the flour into the cap. In reality, as you can see in ⑨, the cupcake rolls unseen into the cap! The spectator holding the cap will feel a pretty big thump, but he'll merely believe it's a big pile of flour landing in his cap. Give the now empty bag a couple of good shakes as you raise it above the cap. Because of the flour that you coated the inside of the bag with, more puffs of flour will emerge around the bag and cap furthering the illusion that flour is everywhere!

Look down into the bag and try to act as if you didn't mean to use quite so much flour. "Oh, I'm sure it'll be fine," you say. A word of caution: Be ready—if at this point he starts to bring the hat down from above his head to take a look, grasp his arm to stop him. If he peeks in now, all is lost.

"Okay, now we need a little milk," you say as you pick up the creamer. Peel back the cover on the creamer and hold its edge just below the rim of the cap as you apparently pour its contents in with the flour ⑩. Raise it up above the cap and shake it a bit, acting like you're trying to get every last drop of milk. Toss the empty container aside.

"And the final ingredient," you say, as you bring forth the egg holding it in your right hand with your thumb over one hole and your first finger concealing the other hole. Try to handle this just as you would a real raw egg. Remind the spectator not to move the cap from above his head, saying, "Please keep the cap nice and still, we don't want to make this any worse."

Make a fist with your left hand and tap the egg on your knuckles (or any other nearby hard surface) to crack it open. Be careful, because it's empty the eggshell is pretty easy to shatter; you just want a small crack. Hold the egg with both hands and press both your thumbs into the crack of the egg. As you begin to crack the egg open, quickly move it up into the cap. Just as you get past the rim of the cap, split the egg open and imitate the actions you'd perform if you were really cracking the egg into the cap . Raise the eggshell halves up and shake them as if your getting the last of the egg glop off them. Toss them aside with the creamer container.

"All that remains is to apply a little heat," you say as you grasp the cap by its bill and take it from the spectator (make sure you hold it so he can't see down inside it). If there is an actual campfire, hold the cap briefly above it (or near it—don't ruin the trick by setting anything on fire, or burning yourself). If there's no fire, hold it over the head of someone with red hair, "The heat coming from this red hair is just right." Failing that, have the assisting spectator rub his hands together under the cap, saying, "The heat generated by this friction is perfect."

"It looks as if it's done," you comment as you sneak a peak into the cap. Ask the spectator to hold his hands cupped in front of him. Slowly turn the cap over, dumping the cupcake into his hands ⑫. As the audience breaks into applause, show that the hat is empty as you brush off any specks of flour and put the hat back on his head. Ta-dah!

I know that's a lot of work for one bit, but trust me, all your work will be handsomely rewarded with loads of laughter and applause for the terrific combination of comedy and mystery this trick creates.

BE PREPARED

 Camping stores sell a plastic container designed to protect eggs on a camping trip. This is a great way to transport the props for this trick, just put a little flour into the flour bag and fold it flat and everything will fit perfectly.

This is not really a trick for you to do one-on-one for your buddy; you need an audience for this one. You want people laughing and going "Eewww!" when you dump the ingredients into the hat.

A biscuit, bagel, or muffin will also work when no cupcake is available. Also, instead of a cap you can make the cupcake in a purse, a hat, or even the outside pocket of someone's jacket.

Keep in mind that while you can do this without the bits of flour coating the inside of the bag and the pinch of flour in the top folds of the bag, seeing those little clouds of flour dust when you open the bag and put the initial pinches into the cap really makes it seem like the bag is full of actual flour. It's little touches like this that make the difference between okay magic and really great magic.

We jump from one of the most elaborate tricks in the book to one of the simplest.

BAFFLING BANDAGE

What They See

A band-aid mysteriously jumps from one of your fingers to another.

What You Need

✔ A band-aid and the usual assortment of fingers (any good camper's first aid kit should contain a few band-aids)

What Really Happens

Before you show the trick wrap the band-aid around the tip of your middle finger ❶. That's it—you're ready to baffle.

When you want to do the trick, hold your hand in front of your body with your two middle fingers extended ❷. Say, "Keep your eye on the band-aid," as you begin waving your hand up and down ❸.

After you've waved for about a second and a half, but while you continue to wave, quickly close your ring finger at the same time stick out your index finger ❹. Don't stop waving immediately—after you've switched fingers keeping waving your hand for another second and a half, gradually slowing down so the audience can see that the band-aid has apparently jumped from one finger to another!

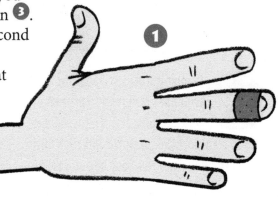

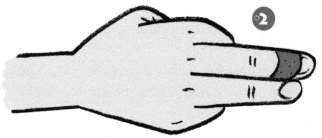

You can make the band-aid jump back by simply reversing the procedure, but I think it's better to quit while you're ahead. A magician never repeats his tricks.

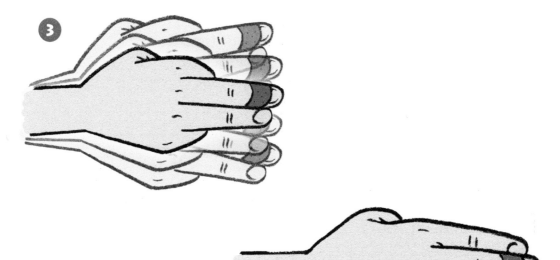

BE PREPARED

 Make sure that when you switch fingers that there is no hesitation in the up and down hand-waving. This is definitely one of those tricks that is aided by practicing in front of a mirror.

Also, I find it helps people follow the effect better if I really spell out what I want them to see by saying, "Watch, the band-aid is on the top finger." Then I do the waving-finger-switching-thing and say, "And now it's on the bottom finger!"

HOLEY SHIRT!

What They See

A pencil penetrates a person's t-shirt without leaving a hole!

What You Need

✔ A small pencil (about four or five inches long is perfect)
✔ A piece of paper approximately eight inches square
✔ An audience of between one and five people, one of whom is wearing a t-shirt

What Really Happens

Believe or not, there is no advance preparation needed for this miracle. Just have the paper and pencil in your pockets. Begin by bringing forth the piece of paper. As you say, "People have lots of theories as to how magic works," fold the paper in half and make a three-quarter-inch tear in the middle of the fold ❶. Unfold the paper and refold it the opposite way and make another three-quarter-inch tear in the middle of that fold ❷ saying, "Some people think all magic is accomplished by using trap doors." Open the paper and poke your finger through the hole you just made ❸ as you say, "They're right."

Ask the person wearing a t-shirt to stand facing you. Have him untuck the shirt if he's the kind of fellow who

actually tucks in his t-shirt. Ask him to hold the bottom of the shirt stretched out between his hands as in ❹. You want there to be about 10 or 12 inches between his hands. If there are other people watching have them help hold the shirt, too. This makes them feel more involved with the trick, but the real reason you have them help hold the shirt is that you want everybody who's watching to be right up next to the action or they might catch a glimpse of the secret dirty work that's going to happen under the shirt. Whoever's holding the shirt, ask them to be sure and not let go, no matter how grisly the upcoming ordeal becomes.

Once the shirt is stretched out and everyone's in position, lay the paper on the t-shirt and say, "The trap door in that piece of paper is the key to the success of this mystery." Then bring forth the pencil and hold it in your right hand near the eraser end as shown in ❺.

Pick up the paper with your left hand, gripping it at one corner with your thumb on top and fingers underneath ❻. Move the paper back to the edge of the shirt as you position the pencil under the shirt and poke the pencil point up and down into the middle of the shirt ❼. Bend over slightly at the waist so that all your attention is intently focused on the center of the shirt. Say, "I'm gonna shove this pencil up through the shirt, right here. Normally this would leave a horrible hole."

Move the paper over the shirt so that the little trap door is directly above the shape of the pencil point pushing up the cloth ❽, as you say, "But because of the magic of the trap door. . . ." Pausing mid-sentence, you now perform three actions simultaneously. One: You move both of your hands back toward the edge of the shirt, and under cover of the shirt and the paper you transfer the pencil from your right hand to the fingers of your left hand (❾ shows this transfer in a super-secret x-ray view). Two: You stand up straight and look up at the owner of the shirt, thus directing attention away from your hands and their secret procedure. Three: You finish your sentence, ". . . it won't leave a hole in your shirt."

Once you've made the secret transfer your right hand immediately goes back to the center of the shirt and begins poking its forefinger up and down into the middle of the shirt as if your finger were the pencil ❿ as you bend slightly forward again focusing your attention on the center of the shirt.

Say, "It's going to go right through here."

Your left hand with the pencil concealed under the paper moves back to its position over the center of the shirt. Your right hand grasps the eraser end of the pencil through the cloth of the shirt as you ask, "Are you ready?" (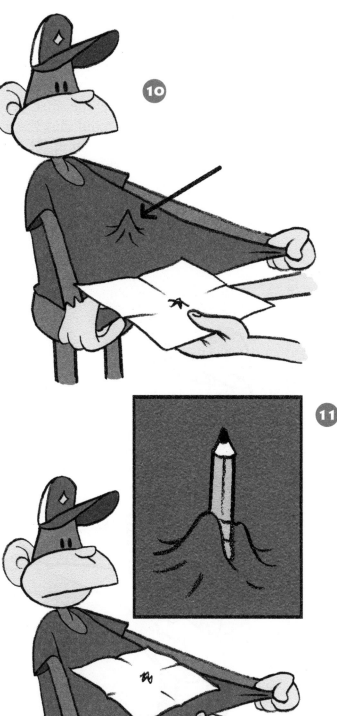 **11** shows the situation just after the right hand has taken the pencil from the left—the paper has been made transparent for clarity.)

As you say, "Don't let go of the shirt" you let go of the paper so that it lays flat on the shirt as your left hand gestures briefly to the spectator's hands holding the shirt. This gives your audience a great picture of the piece of paper isolated in the center of the shirt **12**. This also serves to put a little time between the secret action and the "moment of magic."

Your left hand points to the center of the paper as you say, It's going to come right through there."

Place your left fingers on either side of the hole in the paper as your right fingers push the pencil point up through the hole in the paper . Say, "There it goes! "

Grasp the pencil point with your left hand and pull it up through the paper and (apparently) the shirt. Leave the paper in place on the shirt as your left hand puts the pencil in your pocket or behind your ear to get it out of the way. Bring your right hand out from under the shirt turning it palm up so that everyone sees it's empty. As you slowly pick up the paper with your right hand, rub the shirt with your left hand as you say, "And because of the magic trap door, your shirt is unharmed!"

BE PREPARED

As I mentioned, this is not really a trick for a formal show. It's best to do this for three or four friends standing around. If there was a larger audience they might be able to see under the shirt and your mystery would be spoiled.

You may be wondering why I've put this trick in the "Gear Up" section of the book. That's because if you're careful and responsible you really should do this trick with a small pocketknife instead of a pencil. Aha!

Another variation: Try this when you're playing miniature golf and use the scorecard for the paper and the little pencil they give you.

Regardless of which variation you perform, because of the trickiness of coordinating all the movements required to secretly get the pencil (or knife) from under the center of the shirt to above the center of the shirt without arousing suspicion, this trick is one of the hardest in the book. But I promise that if you master the timing and misdirection needed for this feat, you will be far ahead of most other magicians.

The connection to scout gear is obvious with this next one.

BAFFLING BOLO

What They See

In this goofy sight-gag, the handsome bolo tie you're wearing with your scout uniform mysteriously grows longer and longer until it reaches all the way to the floor!

What You Need

✔ A bolo tie (if this is to be done at a scout meeting you'll want one of the fine-looking ones with scout insignias)
✔ 10 feet of thick string that looks like it could be the cord of a bolo tie (there are jewelry making and macramé cords from the craft store that work great)
✔ You'll also need to be wearing a shirt with a collar that buttons up the front (a scout uniform is perfect—but any shirt you'd wear a bolo tie with will work)

What Really Happens

You can't really stretch your tie using magic, so you'll need to do a bit of advance preparation to bring off this stunt. In order to avoid confusion, in this description I'll refer to the 10 foot long extra cord as "the long cord" and the actual cord that goes with your bolo tie as "the regular cord."

First, you need to do something to spruce up the ends of the long cord. This can be as simple as tying a small knot in each end, or as elaborate as prying loose the actual ends from the

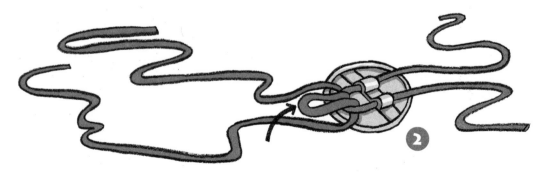

regular cord and fastening them on to the ends of the long cord.

Next, remove the regular cord from your bolo clip and put it back "upside down" so that there is a small loop of cord at the bottom of the clip. The ends of the cord stick out of the top of the clip ❶.

Thread the center of the long cord through the loop of the regular cord that you made at the bottom of the clip ❷.

Next, turn the collar of your shirt up and then tuck all of the middle portion of the long cord down into the neck of your shirt just above the your top button so that only the two ends of the long cord are visible ❸. In order to get the last bit of this long cord tucked in you'll need to raise the bolo clip up to your neck.

Keeping the clip at your neck, tie the ends of the regular cord behind your neck using a regular bowknot ❹. Fold your collar down covering the regular cord. Tuck any exposed ends of the regular cord up under your collar.

When you've completed this setup your tie should look completely normal ❺. If the bolo clip sags down you'll need to retie the regular cord a bit tighter. Once everything looks normal you can head off to your meeting or show.

To make the tie stretch, all you have to do is grasp the ends of the long cord and pull down a bit . You only want to do this a few inches at a time. The idea is that no one ever actually sees the tie stretch. The effect your going for is that over the course of time your time just seems to grow longer. Every time someone looks at you, your tie is just a little longer, but they never actually see it growing. And they never see you yanking on it. You do all of the tugging when no one is looking at you.

If you're doing this in a show, you do the secret yanks when all attention is on an audience member, or when you turn your back to the viewers in order to pick something up. If you're doing this as a gag when you're just hanging out, do the secret pulling when someone else is talking and no attention is on you.

One last little bit, be sure you try this a few time in private so that you can gauge how far to pull the long cord. You don't want to spoil the whole thing by pulling to far and having the entire long cord drop out onto the ground.

BE PREPARED

Every bolo tie slide is different, so you'll need to experiment with the arrangement of the clips, slide, cords, and shirt. To me, that's one of the fun aspects of working on magic tricks; it's really about problem solving. When something's not quite right, you can experiment with different solutions until you find the one that works best for you.

If you're doing the Baffling Bolo trick that means you probably have a neckerchief that you're not wearing. Why not use it in this next trick?

BOUND FOR GLORY

What They See

Explaining that Houdini was a great escape artist who could free himself from any restraint, you offer to demonstrate your own powers of escapology. Even though your wrists are tied together with a bandana, and the bandana is further secured with rope, you manage to escape!

What You Need

✔ A bandana or neckerchief
✔ A five-foot length of rope
✔ A jacket or towel

What Really Happens

Begin by grasping the bandana at diagonally opposite corners and twirling it into a "rope" just as if you were preparing your neckerchief for wearing (❶ illustrates this twirling in progress). Give the bandana to an audience member and ask him to tie one end around your left wrist. Advise him, "Please make it tight enough that I can't slip it off over my hand, but not so tight that it cuts off the blood circulation." Have him tie the opposite end of the bandana around your right wrist the same way.

Once your wrists are securely tied together, have the audience member loop the rope through the bandana between your arms. Ask him to hold the ends of the rope firmly so there is no possibility of you escaping. (❷ shows the position.) Say to the audience, "This is the preferred way to transport prisoners. Except, of course, they use chains instead of bandanas and ropes. If anyone has a length of chain I'd be happy to use that instead." If one of your friends does come forth with chains, you should probably think about getting new friends.

Explaining that you can only escape in the dark, ask someone to cover your hands with their jacket. Once your hands are covered ask for a little slack in the rope as you go into the secret maneuvers that allow you to free yourself. With your right fingers grasp the loop of rope (see ❸ for a view without the covering jacket) and shove it between your left wrist and the bandana ❹.

Pull the loop up and over your left hand ❺. Bring the loop down the back of your left hand and again push it under the bandana at the back of your hand ❻. Once the rope emerges from the bandana, keep pulling and you will suddenly find that you are free! Let the rope drop to the ground and have the audience remove the jacket and examine the bandana to make sure that the knots are still tightly tied. Then run away shouting, "I'm free! I'm free!"

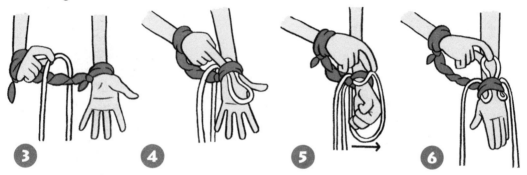

BE PREPARED

Be sure and practice the necessary moves so that you can do them fast enough that it's obvious that you didn't have time to simply untie and retie the knots in the bandana.

If the rope is long enough you can, instead of having your hands covered, simply turn your back to the audience and execute the necessary moves to free yourself. Also, you can use a second piece of rope instead of a bandana if you don't have a bandana or a neckerchief.

If you have two or three bandanas this next one is a good one.

BANDANA SPLIT

What They See

A bandana is tied into a circle. Another bandana is threaded through the first, and tied into a circle so that the two are linked. The connected bandanas are placed into a cap. Magic words are recited and a mystic dance is performed around the cap. At the completion of the bandana ballet, the bandanas are removed from the hat, and while they are still tied in tight circles, they have magically unlinked! By the way, the dance is optional.

What You Need

✔ Two bandanas
✔ A cap

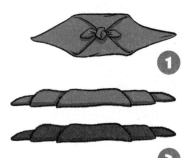

What Really Happens

There's one bit of advance preparation. Lay one of the bandanas out flat and tie two opposite corners together in a nice tight double knot ❶.

Roll up the bandana, hiding the knot inside ❷.

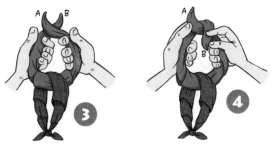

Roll up the second bandana so that it looks like the first, and place the two bandanas in the cap until you're ready to do this trick. If your bandanas are not two different colors don't forget which one is the prepared one!

When you're ready, pick up the cap and its two bandanas. Pick up the unprepared bandana and tie the two ends together in a double knot to form a circle. Thread the second bandana through the first being careful not to let it unroll exposing the hidden knot.

You're going to tie this second bandana in a circle, but you're going to use a trick dissolving knot. I'll break it down and explain this very special knot step-by-step. To make it easier, the description is from your point of view, not the audience's.

Step One: Hold the ends of the bandana like ❸. Throughout the knot-tying process your left and right ring and pinkie

fingers never release their grips on the bandana.
Step Two: Cross end A over end B (see ❸ again).
Step Three: Fold end B down with your right forefinger and thumb ❹.
Step Four: Your right forefinger and thumb let go of end B and grasp end A ❺.
Step Five: Your left forefinger and thumb grasp end B ❻.
Step Six: Tie ends A and B into a single knot ❼.
Step Seven: Pull the knot tight ❽.

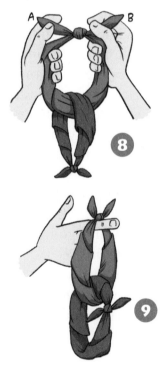

   It looks like you've tied a square knot, but if you pull on the knot at all it will come completely apart. Don't pull on it.
   Hang the two bandanas off your finger displaying their linked condition to the audience ❾, and then place them into the cap. Do your magic hat dance or recite your magic words. Reach into the cap and pull apart the false knot. Then remove the first bandana and display it separate, but still securely tied and hand it to someone to take a look at.
   Reach back into the cap with both hands and spread out the folds of the second bandana to expose the knot then bring it out ❿ showing it still tied in a circle.

Take a well deserved bow!

BE PREPARED

At Step Seven be sure to give the "knot" a number of strong tugs to convince the audience that it's tight. Also, be sure that there is no delay when you reach into the cap and pull out the bandanas. You don't want to generate any suspicion that you had time to untie and retie a knot.

If you have a third bandana you can thread it through the second one and tie it (with a real knot) so that you have three bandanas tied together in a chain with the center one tied with a fake knot. Even though the trick works exactly the same, it somehow seems even more impressive to separate three bandanas.

BODY PARTS

These next few tricks use your actual body as the prop to bring about the magic. Learn a few of these and you'll never be forced to say, "I'd like to do a trick for you but I don't have my equipment with me."

I HAVE 11 FINGERS!

The simplest body trick is to prove that you have 11 fingers instead of the normal allotment of ten. Here are three methods to convince others that you are a genetic oddity.

Method One–Six Plus Five Equals Eleven

"I have eleven fingers!" you happily announce as you hold up your hands displaying all ten fingers 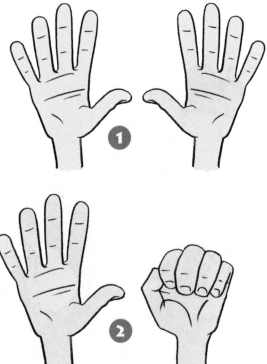. Caution the audience, "Make sure I don't count any fingers more than once." Fold down your left pinkie as you say, "That's ten." Fold down your left ring finger as you say, "Nine." Fold down your left middle finger as you say, "Eight." Fold down your left index finger as you say, "Seven." Fold in your left thumb and display your closed left fist as you say, "Six . . ." Then display your right hand as in ❷, saying ". . . plus these five equals eleven!"

This is the simplest way to show you have eleven fingers, and while it might fool your baby sister, here's a better, more deceptive method. . . .

Method Two–The Power of Eight

"I have eleven fingers!" you weirdly announce as you again hold your hands up displaying all ten fingers spread wide. "In ancient Siamese mythology, eight is the number that influences the hand," you say as you fold your fingers and thumbs in to make fists. You're going to count your fingers saying the word "eight" after every number.

"One-eight," you say as you extend your left thumb 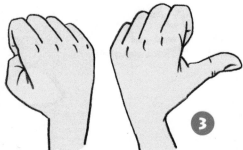. Say, "Two-eight" as you extend your left index finger. Say, "Three-eight" as you extend your left middle finger. Say, "Four-eight" as you extend your left ring finger. Say, "Five-eight" as you extend your left pinkie. Say, "Six-eight" as you extend your right thumb. Say, "Seven-eight" as you extend your right index finger. Say, "Nine-eight" as you extend your right middle finger. Say, "Ten-eight" as you extend your right ring finger. And finally, say, "Eleven-eight" as you extend your right pinkie. Gleefully repeat, "Eleven fingers!"

If you go back and pay attention to what you've said, you'll notice that you don't ever say, "Eight-eight," so you're really sneakily skipping the number eight. Make sure you keep a steady rhythm to your count and this will get past everyone.

Here's the final, and to my mind, best technique.

Method Three—Save These Three

"I have eleven fingers!" you crazily announce as one last time you hold your hands up displaying all ten fingers. This time your palms are facing you.

With your right index finger, fold your left thumb into your palm ④ as you say, "One." Again using your right index finger, fold your left index finger down as you say, "Two." Your right index finger gestures at the remaining three fingers sticking up from your left hand ❺ as you say, "Save these three for later." Keep those three left fingers extended as you, without hesitation, extend all the fingers of your right hand. Look at your right thumb and fold it in as you say, "Four." Fold in your right index finger as you say, "Five." Fold your right middle finger in, saying "Six." Fold in your right ring finger as you say, "Seven." Fold in your right pinkie as you say, "Eight."

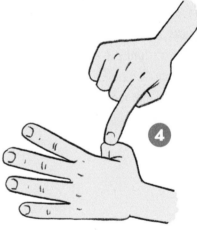

Look at your left hand again (it still has three fingers extended) and fold in your left middle finger as you say, "Nine." Fold in your left ring finger as you say, "Ten." Fold in your left pinkie as you say, "Eleven." Triumphantly exclaim, "I have eleven fingers!"

When you say the phrase, "Save these three for later," you want to place a slight emphasis on the word "three." This distracts attention and helps covers up the fact that you don't ever actually count a third finger.

I have even found that you can actually have the entire audience follow along with their fingers and some of them will still be fooled!

BE PREPARED

You don't have to perform each of these tricks. You can try them a few times and then pick your favorite. You don't have to do these three tricks immediately one after the other. I think it's funny to suddenly announce out of the blue, "I have eleven fingers!" and then do the first method. Twenty minutes (or an hour, or even a day) later you proclaim, "I have eleven fingers!" and then perform the second method. Then twenty minutes, or an hour, or a day later still, you shout, "I HAVE ELEVEN FINGERS!" and then present the third method. Your reputation for eccentricity will be set forever.

YOU CAN'T DO WHAT I DO

What They See

Everyone gathered around the campfire tries to duplicate your apparently simple actions, but no one succeeds.

What You Need

A few people to attempt this feat—the more the better.

✔ Two hands
✔ Ten fingers
✔ Two arms
✔ One nose

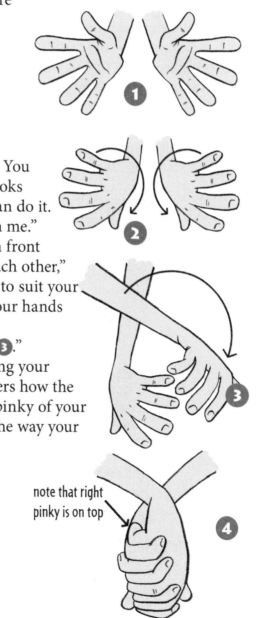

note that right pinky is on top

What Actually Happens

Everyone is gathered 'round the campfire. You say, "I learned something interesting. It looks simple but not one person in a hundred can do it. Here, everybody—try to follow along with me."

Say, "Extend both of your hands out in front of you like this, with your palms facing each other," as you hold your hands out ❶. Continue to suit your actions to your words as you say, "Turn your hands over so that your thumbs point down ❷." "Now cross your right hand over your left ❸."

"Clasp your hands together, interlocking your fingers." Note as you intertwine your fingers how the pinky of your right hand is on top of the pinky of your left hand ❹. For some reason this is not the way your body would naturally clasp your hands together, and it's the key to this whole thing. Believe it or not, everyone else will clasp his or her hands with the left pinky on top.

"Keeping your hands tightly clasped and your fingers interlocked, turn your hands under and up, like this."

Figure 5 clearly shows this action.

"Again, keeping your hands clasped, extend your index fingers."

"With your index fingers crossed, touch your fingernails to your nose, like this 6."

"Keeping your fingertips on either side of your nose, unclasp your hands and straighten your arms, like this." Figure 7 shows this action. Unless they got unaccountably lucky, no one will be able to uncross their hands. They'll be stuck!

Of course it'll happen every now and then that someone accidentally does this correctly. Just congratulate them and say, "You're the one in a hundred who can do this!" Then have them try this next one; there's no way for them to accidentally accomplish it.

YOU STILL CAN'T DO WHAT I DO

What They See

Once again, everyone gathered around the campfire tries to duplicate your actions, but even though this one seems even simpler, still no one succeeds.

What You Need

✔ A few people to attempt this feat—again, the more the better.
✔ Two hands
✔ Ten fingers
✔ Two arms
✔ You don't even need a nose for this one

What Really Happens

You're still gathered 'round the campfire. You say, "Okay, that one was a little tricky. Here's a simpler one. Again, try to follow along with me. It starts out just like the first one."

"Extend both of your hands out in front of you like this, with your palms facing each other," as you hold your hands out as in ❶. As before, suit your actions to your words as you say, "Turn your hands over so that your thumbs point down ❷."

"Now cross your right hand over your left ❸."

"Clasp your hands together, interlocking your fingers ❹."

Pretend to notice that someone hasn't quite got it right as you unclasp your fingers and point to that person with your right hand as you say, "You have to really clasp your hands tight."

note that right pinky is on top

115

Notice in ⑤ how your left hand remains frozen in place as your right hand points.

Next comes the sneaky tricky part. Re-clasp your hands, but this time instead of crossing above your left hand, your right hand rotates a full turn clockwise ⑥ and then reaches under your left hand ⑦. Once again, interlock your fingers ⑧. Wiggle your pinkies as you say, "Keeping your hands tightly clasped together, wiggle your pinkies ⑨. Good. Next, waggle your thumbs. Excellent."

"Now, still keeping your hands tightly clasped together, slowly turn your hands like this." As you say this, you look intently at your hands and little by little rotate them counter-clockwise ⑩, until your arms are completely uncrossed. No one will be able to duplicate your actions without breaking both his arms!

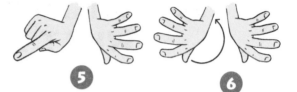

BE PREPARED

Obviously you don't have to do this trick right after the one before it, but they do make a nice tidy little combo.

HOCUS POKE-US

What They See

Touch your index finger and thumb together as in 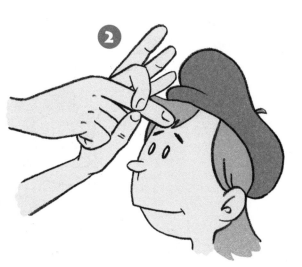. Show this to your friend and ask him if he thinks you can poke his head through this "hole" without separating your fingers. He will state that it is impossible. You prove him wrong in a really funny (and smart aleck-y) way.

What You Need

✔ One hand with at least a finger and thumb
✔ A friend with a good sense of humor

What Really Happens

To poke your friend's head through the hole, simply insert the index finger of your other hand through the hole and poke your friend's head with it . You did it!

BE PREPARED

Keep in mind that you want to imply without saying so that you are somehow going to squish your friend's entire head through the little hole. It helps if, while you are asking your friend if you think you can poke his head through the hole, you hold the hole up to your own head and try to somehow get your head to fit through it.

MIND REWIND

What They See

Have your friend sit down and begin moving her right foot in a clockwise circle on the floor ❶. With her foot still circling, tell her to write the number six in the air with her right finger ❷. Watch as her foot suddenly and uncontrollably starts circling in the opposite direction ❸.

What You Need

A friend with a foot and brain
A place for your friend and her brain to sit down

What Really Happens

There's no real secret to this trick; if your friend follows your instructions this will work!

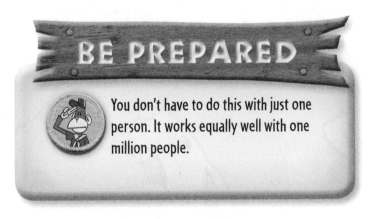

BE PREPARED

You don't have to do this with just one person. It works equally well with one million people.

COIN TRICKS

Coins are great items to do magic with because they're always around and everyone is familiar with them. You can always find a coin. The only trouble is, everybody has a nutty, fumble-fingered uncle who tried to pull a quarter out of his ear and ended up dropping the coin and ruining the trick. But there's more to coin magic than that tired, old gag. Here are a few tricks that will keep you from growing up to be a lame uncle.

THROUGH AND THROUGH

What They See

You display a coin between your right thumb and forefinger. You cover it with a bandana. The coin magically penetrates right through the bandana (without leaving a hole)!

What You Need

✔ A bandana
✔ A coin

What Really Happens

Begin by holding the coin with your right forefinger and thumb ❶. Make sure that everyone sees it. Drape the bandana over the coin and your entire right hand. The center of the bandana is over the coin and the back corner of the bandana rests along your right forearm ❷.

Using your left hand, tuck a little fold of the bandana between the coin and your right thumb (❸ shows this from your point of view).

Your right thumb keeps a grip on the little fold you just made as your left hand grasps the front corner of the bandana and folds it toward the back corner of the bandana. ❹ shows the situation. Notice how your left hand and its corner are directly above the back corner of the bandana. Say, "It's still there," as the coin comes into view.

Your left hand grasps the lower corner of the bandana and folds both corners back over the coin ❺. The audience thinks the coin is inside the bandana, but it's really on the outside. Your right hand holds the center of the bandana folded over the coin (❻ shows the situation from your point of view).

Your left hand grips the coin through the bandana ❼ and slowly pulls the coin through the cloth. From the audience's point of view ❽ it looks like the coin is being pulled right through the center of the bandana!

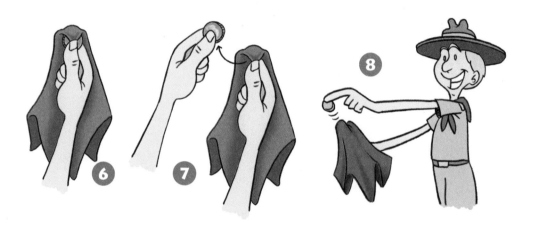

BE PREPARED

I like to pretend to struggle as I pull the coin through the bandana at the end as if it's really difficult. You don't have to use a bandana for this. A napkin or a handkerchief works just fine.

You don't even have to use a coin; if you're camping try it with an Oreo® or a flattish rock.

As a matter of fact, lots of tricks that magicians do with coins are just as good with rocks. This next one is a fine example....

FOLLOW THE MONEY

What They See

The magician asks six people to stand in a line. Handing a folded slip of paper and a coin to a seventh participant, our hero then turns his back. The magician asks the participant to hand the coin to any of the six people in line. He then directs the six people in line to pass the coin from person to person. Even with his back turned, the magician seems to know which person has the coin at every step of the trick. And for the big finish, the folded piece of paper is opened and it correctly names the final person holding the coin at the end of all the passing!

What You Need

✔ Seven people
✔ A coin
✔ A blank piece of paper
✔ A pencil or marker
✔ An index card or small scrap of paper with the these instructions written on it:

FOLLOW THE MONEY

1. MOVE NUMBER OF PERSON
2. PERSON 1 SITS
3. 1 MOVE
4. PERSON 6 SITS
5. 4 MOVES
6. PERSON 2 SITS
7. 3 MOVES
8. PERSON 3 SITS
9. 3 MOVES
10. PERSON 4 SITS
11. PERSON 5 HAS THE ROCK!

What Really Happens

Before the trick, write on the paper, "Try as you might, you can not avoid your destinies. The coin will end up with person number five. It is impossible for it to be otherwise." Fold up this paper with the writing on the inside and put it in your pocket with the coin.

When you're ready to perform this trick, invite six people to stand in a row and assign them numbers one through six in order from left to right. Caution them to remember their assigned numbers. Hand a seventh person the prediction paper and the coin.

Explain the procedure carefully so that everyone understands: "In a moment, I'm going to turn my back and I'll ask you to make a number of 'moves' with the coin. A move consists of handing the coin from one person to the person right next to him—you can't skip over a person. In other words, person number 4 can hand the coin only to person number 3 or 5—he can't hand it to person 2, that would be skipping over person 3. Person 1 can hand it to person 2, but not person 6 or 3. Got it? Excellent." To aid in people understanding these rules, as you're making this explanation you should point to the numbered people as you name them.

Once they understand the rules, turn your back and have the person holding the coin and the prediction choose one of the six people in the line and have her hand the coin to her chosen person. As she's doing that, you slyly remove the index card from your pocket and hold it so you can read it. Notice that the first instruction on the card reads, "Move number of person." This is your cue to say to the helper,

"The coin is now held by a person with an assigned number. Please make as many moves with the coin as that person's number. In other words, if person number 5 holds the coin, you'd make five moves. Or if person number 2 holds the coin you'd make two moves. Go ahead and make your moves now."

After they've completed their moves you consult your cue sheet. It says, "Person 1 sits," so you say, "My highly advanced mental powers tell me that the coin is not now in the possession of person number 1. Person number 1 please sit down. Once a person sits down, you can no longer hand them the coin."

The next line on the instruction sheet reads "1 move," so you say, "Now, make one move."

When they've made the move you consult the next line of the instruction sheet. It reads, "Person 6 sits," so you say, "My super senses say that person 6 does not now have the coin. Person 6, please sit down. Remember, once a person sits down you can no longer hand them the coin."

Continue following the instruction sheet so that the participants make 4 moves, person 2 sits down, they make three moves, person 3 sits, they make three moves, and person 4 sits.

Say, "That leaves one person standing; person number 5, and that's who holds the coin!" Turn and face the audience as you continue, "Not only that, but take a look at the prediction I gave you before any of this began." Have the prediction holder open the paper and read it aloud. Spooky!

BE PREPARED

Remember that the idea you're trying to get across is that even though the participants have a great deal of freedom in how they pass the coin, you are able to tell where it is at every step. You want them to believe that this is a feat of mindreading and not simply some mathematical certainty.

Again, this doesn't have to be done with a coin. A rock, or a neckerchief slide, or any small object works great. And while it doesn't really matter if someone sees the index card you're reading the instructions from, I think it's best to try and keep it hidden. Anyway, once you've done this a few times you'll probably have the instructions memorized and won't even need them.

This trick is based on one I first learned from Karl Fulves *Self-Working Coin Magic*. Mr. Fulves has a whole series of these Self-Working books, and they're all loaded with great tricks.

And speaking of "self-working," once you've made up the necessary props, this next one practically works itself.

MONEY FOR NOTHIN'

What They See

You show a dollar bill front and back, roll it into a tube, and dump out a shiny new penny. "The problem is," you say, "there's no such thing as a free lunch. That penny had to come from somewhere." When you unroll the dollar there is a neat penny-sized piece missing from the dollar.

What You Need

✔ Two one-dollar bills that you can afford to not spend
✔ A penny
✔ A pencil
✔ Scissors
✔ White glue

What Really Happens

In order to do this without any sleight of hand, one of the dollar bills is pretty tricked out. Here's how you do this little arts and crafts project. With the first dollar bill face down, place a penny near the lower right corner and draw a circle around it with the pencil. Cut out the circle with the scissors leaving that first dollar with a penny sized hole in it ❶.

From the second dollar neatly and carefully cut out the circle around the pyramid on the back left side ❷. Put the rest of that second dollar aside; all you need for this is the circle.

Put a thin bit of glue on the bottom edge of the back of the circular pyramid piece (❸ shows exactly where to apply the glue). Glue that piece to the back of the first dollar directly over the matching spot, so that it lines up perfectly, and makes a little secret pocket. Wipe away any

excess glue that seeps out, and set the
dollar aside to dry. When the glue is
good and set, your preparation is done.
You've created a dollar with a penny-
sized hole in one half and a secret
pocket in the other half ④.

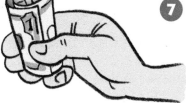

Before you show this trick to
anyone, slide the penny down into the
secret pocket. You're ready to mystify.

Bring forth the dollar holding it with
George Washington right side up and
facing the audience. Your right fingers
conceal the hole from view ⑤. Using
your right thumb, curl the right side of
the dollar toward the left, so that the
hole is hidden behind the center of the
bill ⑥. Continue curling the bill until it
is rolled into a loose tube about one inch
across ⑦. Keep the tube from unrolling
by holding it lightly between your right
thumb and forefinger.

Tilt the tube up so the open bottom
end of the tube and both of your palms are
toward the audience ⑧. Don't tilt too far
or the penny will fall out of the top of the
tube! Pause in that position as you say, "A
small tube and two empty hands."

Your left hand turns palm up at the same time as your
right hand returns the tube to its upright position as you
say, "And yet. . . ."

Slowly and
deliberately tilt
the tube over the
spectator's open
hand so that the
penny slides forth
from its secret
pocket and drops
into his palm ⑨.

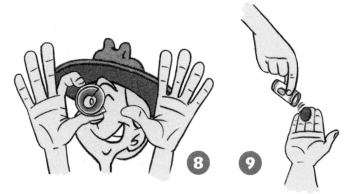

Finish by saying, "The problem is, there's no such thing as a free lunch. That penny had to come from somewhere." Unroll the dollar to reveal that there is now a penny-sized hole in the dollar .

BE PREPARED

If you want to do this without the spectator, you can dump the penny into your own hand or onto the table. However you do it, you just want to make sure that the audience clearly sees the penny emerge from the tube you just showed empty.

Now that you've got some easy coin tricks under your belt, it's time to learn one that actually takes some sleight-of-hand (that's magician-talk for magic that requires skilled hand movements).

POROUS PALM

What They See

You clearly and distinctly count seven coins into someone's hand. He quickly closes his fingers making a tight fist around the coins. Despite the strength of his grip, and his determination to keep you out, you are able to magically remove one of the coins from his hand!

What You Need

✔ Seven pennies (or small rocks)

What Really Happens

Begin by extending your left hand and displaying the seven pennies on your palm . Indicate one person from the onlooking multitudes as you say, "I have seven pennies. I need you to help me with a little experiment." Ask the chosen person to hold his right hand out palm-up.

Say, "I'm going to count these pennies one at a time into your hand. As soon as the seventh penny touches your hand I want you to close your hand as quickly and as tightly as you can. Got it? As soon as the seventh penny hits your hand, close it as quickly as you can. Ready?"

Pick up one of the pennies with your right hand with your fingers in front and your thumb in back (❷ shows the grip). Place the penny into the outstretched palm of the volunteer as you count, "One." ❸ shows how you put the penny in his hand; you're placing it, not tossing or throwing it.

Pick up a second penny from your hand (holding it the same way—so that most of the penny is hidden behind your right fingers) and place it next to the first one, counting, "Two." Pick up and place the third penny, counting, "Three." Pick up and place the fourth penny, counting "Four." Pick up and place the fifth penny counting, "Five." Pick up and place the sixth penny counting, "Six."

The seventh penny is handled differently. After placing the sixth penny into the volunteer's hand, your right hand moves toward your belly out of the way ④. As soon as your right hand moves away, your left hand rotates at the wrist and drops the seventh coin into the helper's hand (see ⑤ for an in-flight view of the coin dropping). Say, "Seven," as you dump the last coin. If necessary, urge him to close his hand quickly.

After he's closed his hand on the seven coins, either compliment him on how quickly he closed his hand, or remind him that the next time he needs to close his hand quicker. Explain that that was just the set up, so he could practice closing his hand quickly and tightly. Ask him to open his hand and count them out loud as he places the pennies one at a time back into your palm up left hand. Having the spectator count the pennies helps to firmly establish that there are, in fact, seven pennies.

When he finishes counting say, "This time it's for real. I'm going to count these seven pennies one at a time back into your hand. Remember, as soon as the seventh penny touches your hand I want you to close your hand as quickly and as tightly as you can. Don't let any thing in or out. Are you ready?"

This count should look exactly like the practice run you did. Begin by pick up one of the pennies with your right

hand (remember—fingers in front and your thumb in back). Place the penny into the outstretched palm of the volunteer as you count, "One." Pick up a second penny from your hand and place it next to the first one counting, "Two." Pick up and place the third penny, counting, "Three." Pick up and place the fourth penny, counting "Four." Pick up and place the fifth penny counting, "Five."

On the sixth penny you do the dirty work. Pick up the sixth penny so that it is hidden behind your right fingers and place it onto the spectator's palm just as you did the first five. But this time don't let go of the penny. That's right, just touch the penny to the pile of five pennies already there, say, "Six," and then move your right hand out of the way toward your belly (again, you're duplicating the actions from the practice run). Without delay, dump the last penny from your left hand into the helper's hand as you say, "Seven."  is an exposed view of what's going on at this crucial moment. He should immediately close his hand tightly around the coins. If he forgets, remind him to do so.

coin hidden

As you dump the seventh coin and he's closing his hand you relax your entire right arm, allowing it to fall to your side. The stolen coin contained in your right hand remains concealed in your loosely closed fingers. Focus all of your, and the spectator's, attention on the closed fist of the helper. Caution him to keep his fist tightly closed.

Now, for the first time, you reveal the true point of the trick. Close your empty left hand into a fist as you say, "You have seven coins held tightly in your fist. Please turn your hand over like this." Demonstrate what you mean with your left hand.  shows the helper in mid-turn as he follows your direction. You continue, "The idea is I am going to try to reach through the flesh and bones of the back of your hand and magically remove one of the coins. Don't worry, this is completely painless—to me."

Bring your right hand up and rest it on the back of the volunteer's closed fist, making sure the coin remains hidden from view in your curled fingers.

Lightly pinch the back of the helper's fist between your right fingers and palm. Don't pinch hard, you're not trying to hurt him, you just want him to feel you slightly gripping his skin .

Pull your right hand up and turn it over as you open it **9** to dramatically reveal the coin you pulled through his flesh!

To finish, have him open his hand and count the remaining coins. Six!

 This trick teaches you an important lesson in what us magicians call "misdirection." Misdirection is when you turn people's attention from what you don't want them to notice by getting them to focus their interest on something else.

In this trick you misdirect the volunteer's attention from the secret taking of the sixth penny by directing his mind to the dumping of the seventh penny into his hand. If you do this right it is impossible for any of the people watching to keep their eyes on your right hand doing its dirty work. They are forced to switch their concentration to your left hand and the falling penny. This is partly because their eyes are attracted to the movement of the

left hand turning to dump the seventh coin, and partly because their eyes are attracted to the flight of the coin as it falls. This is also helped considerably by the fact that you have commanded the helper to quickly close his hand as soon as the last coin touches his palm. You have made the seventh coin's journey extremely important in everyone's mind. The sixth coin isn't nearly as important, so all attention is directed from the sixth coin to the seventh.

Once you master this trick, you will amaze yourself with this ability to control people's attention with misdirection. Understanding misdirection and being able to apply it to every trick you do, is yet another step toward becoming a master magician.

THE BUDDY SYSTEM

One of the ways I recommend to get good at magic is to have a "magic buddy," a pal who's also interested in magic. That way you can watch and help each other work on your tricks. You'll need to trust one another to be honest with both criticism and praise. You'll both get better quicker. For the tricks in this section, though, your pal doesn't have to be a magician at all. All his work is simple and takes little or no rehearsal. . . .

THE LAST PERSON YOU'D EXPECT

What They See

You borrow a coin and hold it in your outstretched palm-up hand. Then you cover your hand and the coin with a bandana. A few people even feel under the bandana to make sure the coin is still there. When everyone's satisfied that the coin is still there on your hand, without any false moves, you whisk away the bandana to show that the coin has disappeared!

What You Need

✔ A bandana (a neckerchief, handkerchief, or napkin will also work)
✔ A coin—preferably borrowed
✔ A pal who's secretly in on the trick

What Really Happens

Begin by borrowing the coin. The larger the denomination the better. Display the coin on the palm of your hand. Cover the coin with the bandana, "To lend and air of mystery."

Lift up the front edge of the bandana and ask one of the audience members to reach under the cloth and "Make sure the coin is still there." She affirms that it is.

Ask a couple of other people to reach under and satisfy themselves that the coin remains there on your hand. The last person you request to feel the coin is your secret helper pal. When he reaches under to check out the coin, he simply picks up the coin and withdraws his hand with the coin concealed in it as he says, "Yup. It's still there."

You then say, "You've seen the coin, you've felt the coin. You know the coin is there, my sleeves are rolled up so there's absolutely no place for the coin to go, and yet, watch, as the coin melts away!" You whip the bandana off your hand so that they can see the coin is gone. Toss the bandana into the air so that they realize that it too is empty. The coin seems to have truly disappeared.

 Make sure that when you remove the bandana that you allow the audience to see that your hand is in fact empty. There's no need to rush. You've got no coin hidden anywhere so you can afford to slowly and deliberately show both your hands and the bandana are completely empty.

If you wish, you can bring the coin back by basically following the same procedure in reverse. Cover your hand with the bandana. Have people reach under and feel your palm to make sure your hand is empty. Your helper is the last one to reach under. This time he secretly leaves the coin in your hand. However, if you decide not to make the coin reappear, you've made a small profit. My rule of thumb is: if I borrow the coin from a kid I magically bring it back, if I borrow it from an adult, I keep it.

Next is another one where the audience isn't aware that your pal is in on the trick. Only this time it's comedy instead of mystery that is your goal.

CUT THE CARDS

What They See

During the course of your show, you invite a random audience member up to help you, hand him a deck of cards, and tell him, "Please cut the cards." Imagine the laughter and surprise when he picks up a pair of scissors ❶ and begins cutting the cards in half one at a time!

What You Need

✔ A friend
✔ A pair of scissors
✔ An old deck of cards you don't mind ruining

What Actually Happens

Before the show you've arranged with your friend what he is to do. You invite him up, hand him the deck and ask him to cut the cards. You step forward toward the audience and begin telling them about your next feat of amazing card magic. Make sure that he understands that he is to wait until you step forward to speak to the audience and he is out of your sight, and then he should apparently notice the scissors and grab them from your bag of props and start cutting the

cards in half one at a time. Also make sure he holds the cards and scissors so that the audience can see his act of destruction. There's no laugh if no one sees his act of destruction.

Look puzzled at why the audience is reacting with laughter to your speech about your upcoming card miracle. Stop talking and then look around apparently "catching" the culprit in mid snip. Pretend to get mad at him. Take the scissors out of his hand (be careful) and ask him to please take his seat. Get someone else up and continue with a legit card trick, staring intently at the volunteer when you ask her to cut the cards. One of the Predict-O-Matic card tricks would be good here, since they all begin with having the cards cut in a more conventional style.

The goal here is for the audience to not realize that your friend is in on the gag. You want them to think that you simply invited someone up to help with a card trick and they spotted your scissors and got it in their head to take your request literally and actually start hacking the cards in half.

I think it's best if you've already used the scissors in a trick so the audience is already aware that the scissors are there among your props, but this isn't critical.

In the previous tricks the audience is unaware of your secret helper. In this next one, he's right out in the open.

BLACK MAGIC

What They See

You introduce your costar by explaining that he has telepathic abilities developed by years spent in isolation in his bedroom. Your psychic assistant goes behind a tree (or into a tent— anywhere he can't observe the proceedings) and the remaining people quietly choose any object in the area. You ask them to focus their minds on that object but not to betray its identity by staring at it or giving any other sign. When the object has been chosen, you call your assistant back, saying that he will discover the selected article by using the energy from the collective brainpower of the group concentrating on that object.

You begin pointing at various items, each time simply asking the mind reader, "Is that it?" He continuously responds, "No" until you point at the chosen object whereupon he says, "Yes, that's it."

Of course your audience will think that this is merely a trick of some sort and that you are somehow signaling him, so you offer to repeat the experiment. Again the psychic is correct. *After* seeing this a third and fourth time without observing any secret signals your friends are forced to conclude that your friend is indeed psychic.

What Actually Happens

Your friend is not actually psychic (no matter how much time he actually spends isolated in his bedroom), so you do have to secretly signal him. You tell your friend privately before the trick that the first thing you point to after you point to something black in color will be the chosen object. That's it; just like all psychic occurrences it's just a simple trick. But don't the simplicity of this secret prevent you from trying this out. Simplicity is really the key to good magic.

BE PREPARED

Even though I've described this trick as if you're outdoors, you can easily do this inside; just have the pretend psychic leave the room while the object is being chosen.

Most of the time I would caution you not to repeat the same trick for the same audience. The second time you do a trick, the audience anticipates the ending and thus has some idea of what to look for. But this is the rare trick which actually becomes more mysterious and puzzling the more it is repeated.

The main reason to repeat this trick is that people will think of various theories as to how you're accomplishing this feat and you should do your best to counter each of them. For example, you should always say exactly the same words, "Is that it?" That way folks won't think that your words somehow convey hidden information to the supposed psychic. Also, you don't want people to think that the correct object is always the fifth one you point to, so make sure you vary the number of objects you point to before you point to the correct one. And don't use the same black item as your cue.

So, having said that it's a good idea to perform this trick more than once, I feel the need to caution you to not repeat this too many times. Learn to be a good judge of the mood of the audience by listening to them and deciding when you've done enough.

In this next one the audience is aware of your magic buddy, but they never actually see him.

PHONEY WIZARD

What They See

You spread the deck out face-up and someone randomly selects a card. Mentioning that you have a friend who specializes in long distance mindreading, you give him a call on the phone. Even though he is miles away he manages to guess the freely chosen card.

What You Need

✔ A deck of cards
✔ A friend who is not present at your performance and has a phone and is willing to learn his part of the trick
✔ Access to a phone (yours or someone else's)

What Really Happens

Obviously the long distance mindreader is in on the trick. You communicate the card to him via a secret code, but don't worry, it's really easy.

Once the audience has selected a card you call your secret pal. When he answers, you say, "Hello, is the Wizard there?" This alerts your friend that you've called to do this trick. Your friend immediately begins to slowly name the suits of the cards. He says, "Clubs," pauses a beat, then says, "Hearts," pauses

a beat, and then says, "Spades," pauses a beat, and then says "Diamonds." As soon as you hear him say the suit of the chosen card you say to the audience (but loud enough that the Wizard can hear over the phone), "I'm on hold." Your pal knows that the suit of the card is the last one he had a chance to name before you interrupted him.

As soon as you say, "I'm on hold," your friend begins to recite the values of the card. He says, "Ace," pauses a beat, then says, "Two," then pauses a beat, "Three," pause, "Four" pause, "Five," pause, "Six," pause, "Seven," pause, "Eight," pause, "Nine," pause, "Ten," pause, "Jack," pause "Queen," pause, "King." As soon as he says the value of the selected card you interrupt him again, "Hello, Wizard? Can you read someone's mind today?" He knows the value of the card is the last one he had a chance to say before you interrupted him.

You hand the phone to the person who selected the card. If the phone you're using to call the Wizard has a speakerphone function, you can turn it on now so that everyone can hear the Wizard as he says, "Hello, this is the great Wizard. Did you wish to know something? Have you chosen an object for the Wizard to identify?"

The person holding the phone answers, "Yes."

The Wizard says in a hesitant manner, "Please concentrate on the object. I'm getting the sense that it's small and rectangular…and made of paper. Is it a playing card?"

"Yes"

The Wizard states, "I'm getting the sense that there's more. You'd like me to tell you exactly which card it is. Is that correct?"

"Yes."

The Wizard requests, "Please concentrate on the card. Are there other people there with you? Please ask them to all try to send me the thought of the card… I'm getting a black card. Is that correct?"

"Yes."

The Wizard continues, "It's a spade. Not a high value, but not really low, either. I believe it is the five of spades." The Wizard hangs up without saying goodbye.

BE PREPARED

If the code seems a tad confusing, here's a sample of how the part of your conversation where you secretly disclose the name of the card to the Wizard would go if in fact the chosen card was the Five of Spades.

You: "Hello, is the Wizard there?"

Wizard (realizing you called to do the trick): "Clubs... Hearts ... Spades...."

You: "I'm on hold." Because you spoke after he said "Spades" the Wizard knows the chosen card is a Spade.

Wizard: "Ace ... Two ... Three ... Four ... Five ...."

You: "Hello, Wizard? Can you read someone's mind today?" Because you spoke after he said "Five" the Wizard knows the chosen card was a Five.

Your friend who plays the Wizard should disguise his voice as much as possible and maybe even speak with a foreign accent if he can pull it off. Nothing is worse than having someone pipe up in the middle of the Wizard's dialogue, "That's not a Wizard, that's just your friend Pete!"

If someone in the audience gets the bright idea that they should hit redial on the phone to ask the Wizard another question (if you do this often enough, it's almost certain that this will happen), instruct the Wizard that if he doesn't recognize your voice he should say that the Wizard is meditating and cannot be disturbed.

You don't even really need an actual deck of cards to do this. You can tell an audience member, "Imagine that you have an entire deck of 52 cards spread out in front of you. I want you to run your mind's eye over the spread and name any one of the cards you see." Or can just have the audience agree on any playing card. As long as you know the name of the chosen card you can secretly transmit it to your friend.

Notice how the Wizard asks, "Have you chosen an object you'd like me to identify?" instead of "Have you chosen a card for me to identify?" This makes it sound like he could have identified anything in the world–instead of merely one of 52 cards. Much more impressive.

IT'S NOT REALLY MAGIC, BUT...

Sometimes the mood just isn't right for magic, or maybe your friends are tired of your trickery (I know, that seems impossible), either way you can still amuse them with a few cool puzzles and stunts.

ROCK STAR

What They See

You've had an adventurous day of hiking and you're kicking back relaxing with you pals. The talk turns to cool rock formations that you saw on your hike. "Speaking of rock formations," you say, "Here are 10 rocks. Your mission is to lay them out on the ground in five rows so that there are four rocks in each row. And you can't stack one rock on top of another, that's cheating. "

What You Need

✔ 10 small rocks

What Really Happens

Once they've given up, you lay out the rocks in the shape of a five-pointed star with rocks at each point and at each of the line intersections. ❶ will make this much clearer than my words.

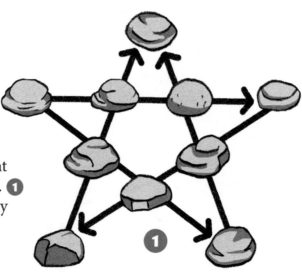

BE PREPARED

If you're feeling bold, you can say to the challengee while she's struggling to figure this out: "If you get this, you'll be a rock star." You'll have to read the person and decide if that's too much of a hint.

Obviously you don't have to do this with rocks. You can use coins, sugar packets, or any other small objects that you have handy.

MYSTERY MATCHES

What They See

Every well-stocked pack of any scout should contain some dry matches. Once your campfire is safely started you can amuse your friends with these devious brainteasers.

What You Need

✔ A bunch of matches

What Really Happens

These aren't really tricks they're actually puzzles. For each one, just lay out the matches as diagramed, and state the problem simply so that everyone understands what needs to be accomplished.

The secret to presenting these is to avoid making them offensive; don't challenge people or try to make yourself out as superior. The idea is that you are sharing something fun and interesting. You want to leave people with the feeling that they've learned something cool that they can show their other friends.

Keep in mind that all these puzzles can also be done with toothpicks, crayons, or even small sticks. Remember, as well, these are supposed to be fun for people to fiddle with together, don't be mean if someone can't figure them out!

1. Lay out matches likes this. . .
Say to your friend, "Please remove 5 matches and leave 3 squares."

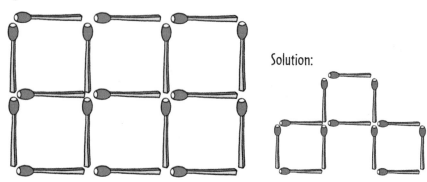

2. Lay out 12 matches like this. . .
Say to your friend, "Remove just 2 matches and leave 2 squares."

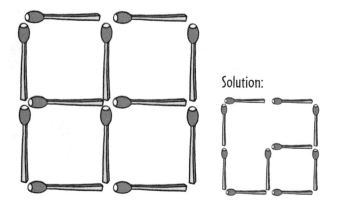

3. Challenge your pal to make 10 square's with 15 matches (without breaking any matches).
When she has tried everything, lay the matches out like this. . .
(At first glance this is only 8 squares, but there are two larger squares–each made of 4 smaller squares.)

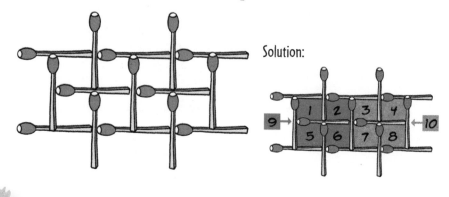

4. Lay out matches like this. . .
Say to your friend, "Arrange these ten matches to form 5 triangles."

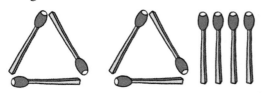

When they give up, do this. . .

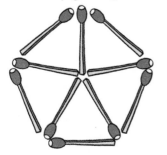

5. Give your friend 8 matches and ask him to make 2 squares and 8 triangles (as always, no breaking the matches).

Here's how to do it:

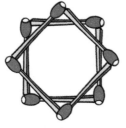

6. Arrange 4 matches like this. Also, put down a little wad of paper. Say that this is your glass of milk with a fly in it. Challenge your friend to get the fly out by moving only 2 matches and without touching the fly.

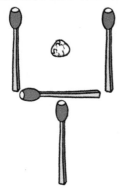

Move the 2 matches like this, you've turned your glass upside down, and now the fly is out!

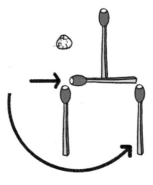

RECYCLED PAPER

What They See

Recycling and the environment are important to all campers and scouts. Using only his bare hands, our champion recycler transforms a few sheets of plain newspaper into a tree!

What You Need

✔ 4 to 6 full-sized sheets of newspaper
✔ A rubberband
✔ A pair of scissors (optional)

rubber band about six inches from the bottom

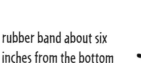

What Really Happens

Lay out a sheet of newspaper as in. Starting at the narrow edge, begin rolling the sheet into a roll about an inch or so in diameter, as in. When you reach the crease in the center of the paper, pause and lay a second sheet of newspaper overlapping the first . Keep rolling the newspaper until you get to the fold in the center of the second sheet. Lay down the third sheet overlapping the unrolled part of the second sheet. Keep repeating this pattern of rolling and laying down sheets until you've used up all your newspaper sheets. When you're finished rolling, snap the rubberband around the roll about 6 inches from the bottom to keep the whole thing from coming apart ❷.

Squish the top end of the paper cylinder sort of flat ❸ so that you can tear it down the middle ❹. You'll need to tear the paper slowly, an inch or two at a time, to get a good straight tear. Stop tearing when you get about halfway down. Flatten the torn strips together ❺ and tear them in half. The top portion of the paper tube will now

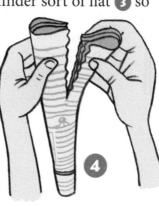

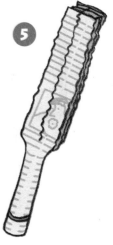

be torn into four sections with each section made up of a bunch of torn strips.

Bend each of the four torn sections out from the center of the tube ❻. Hold the tube at its base (near the rubberband) with your left hand and reach down into the center of the top of the tube and grip the inner layer of paper with your right fingers at the base of the tears you made. As you grasp the paper you can say, "Paper is made from trees, and trees are a precious natural resource. Wouldn't it be great if we could transform paper back into trees?"

Pull the center of the paper out saying, "Well, we can!" The paper will spiral up as you continue to pull it out, making a tree ❼.

BE PREPARED

If the layers of paper are too thick to tear with your hands, you can use scissors.

Should you wish to get really ambitious, handing out four or five sheets of newspaper and a rubberband to everyone in the audience and having them follow along with you can create an amazing spectacle. Everyone makes a tree. When everyone's tree is extended, take out your camera and snap a photo of the wondrous "forest" they've magically created.

If you find that both you and your audiences like this paper tree bit, here's a cute follow up. . . .

UP THE LADDER

What They See

You roll up a bunch of newspaper sheets and tear out a small section. The paper expands into a ladder!

What You Need

✔ Four to six full-sized sheets of newspaper
✔ Two rubber bands
✔ A pair of scissors (optional)

What Really Happens

You roll up the newspaper sheets just like in the previous trick, and slip the rubber bands around the cylinder about three inches from each end. Then you tear away a section from the center of the newspaper tube ❶.

Fold the two ends of the tube down and hold them together in your left hand ❷.

tear section out like this

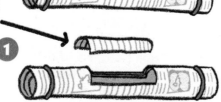

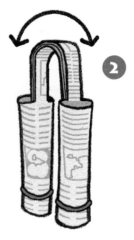

With your right hand, grasp the torn center and pull it up
3. Keep pulling and extending until it won't go any higher.

Grasp one half in each hand and separate your hands **4** so that a ladder forms!

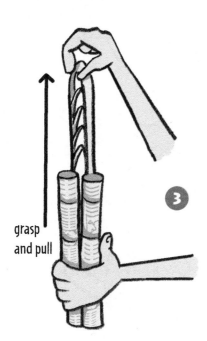

grasp
and pull

BE PREPARED

You can use this as a follow up feat to "Recycled Paper" by saying, "You know, the best fruit on a paper tree (point at the paper tree you just completed) is at the top. Do you know the best way to get to the top of a paper tree? A paper ladder, of course!"

CHAPTER 10
ROUTINE MAGIC

Magicians refer to the stringing together of a few magical effects to make a longer trick as a "routine." I thought that once you get good at doing the separate tricks from the earlier chapters of this book, you might want to try your hand at one of these more complicated routines. This last chapter gives you a detailed description of one of my favorites.

A COMEDY MAGIC ACT

What They See

You begin by borrowing a dollar from someone and folding it into quarters. "Is this the dollar you gave me?" you ask him as you hold it up. When he replies in the affirmative you say, "Thank you," and put the dollar in your pocket.

"Just kidding," you say as you withdraw the dollar and fold it one more time and place it under a table leg. "There. That's much better. It doesn't wobble anymore," you state as you give the table a little shake to test its stability.

"Now, does anyone have a handkerchief or bandana I could borrow?" Someone holds up a bandana. You take it and say thank you as you blow your nose in it with a loud snort. You look at the bandana, decide you like it, and put it into your pocket.

"Now for some magic," you say as you take out a deck of cards. "Would you please help me? Please take any card," you request as you fan the cards out and approach a spectator. Just as he's about to reach for one, a card magically shoots out of the deck and lands at his feet. "Oh, you dropped it," you say as you put the deck aside and bend down and pick up the card.

"You've freely chosen the Six of Hearts," you say as you show the card to the other spectators. Hand the card to the spectator and instruct him, "We're going to do a very special trick with that card. I know this is going to seem weird, but don't worry, it'll all work out in the end. I want you to tear the card in half…" as soon as he tears the card in half, you finish the sentence by saying, "…mentally." You look at him as if he's completely ruined your trick and then smile and say, "No that's fine. Now tear those two pieces in half so the card is in quarters, and then tear those pieces one more time so that you have eight pieces of card."

Retrieving the pieces from the spectator, you hand him back one of the corners of the torn card as you say, "Wait, you should keep one of the pieces." You then put a rubber band around the remaining pieces and have him hold those as well.

"Actually," you say as you remove the bandana from your back pocket, "Because what is about to happen to those seven pieces of card is so frightening, maybe we should blindfold them." So you take the rubber-banded pieces of card and wrap them in the bandana and ask him to hold them in his free hand (the hand not holding the single piece of card you gave him earlier).

Next you remove an egg from your pocket, holding it up for all to see. "Over there, the card. Over here, the egg. Over there, the torn pieces. Here, the egg." As you say these words, you look more and more intently at the egg. Distracted by its egg-y goodness, you break open its shell revealing that it is hardboiled. Then you reach under your shirt and take out a paper plate. You peel the egg completely and, apparently overcome with hunger, you take a bite from the egg. Resting the egg on the plate you reach into your pocket and take out a saltshaker, shake a little salt onto the egg, and then continue taking bites of the egg and chewing in silent oblivion until you've eaten the entire egg.

Looking up and noticing the audience watching you, you look a little sheepish. "Oh, yes. The card in the egg trick." Realizing that you no longer have an egg, you ask, "Does anyone have an egg I could borrow? No? Well I guess we won't be doing the card in egg trick today."

You look around desperately for an object that the card could magically appear in. Spotting the saltshaker you say, "Aha! The card in the saltshaker trick!" Hold up the saltshaker with one hand and then grasp one corner of the bandana with you other hand. Ask the person holding the bandana, "Can you feel the pieces of card inside there?" After he says that he can in fact feel the pieces, you hesitate a moment and then say, "They're gone!" as you whisk the bandana from his grasp. The pieces have vanished!

Tossing the bandana aside, you slowly unscrew the cap of the saltshaker. Then you pour the salt onto the plate revealing that there is a folded object in the midst of the pile of salt. "What's that?" you exclaim as you hold the plate out to the spectator.

"Is it a card?" you ask, as he picks up and opens up the folded item. "No. It's a note," he replies.
"A note? Please read it aloud," you request.

He reads, "I-O-U one dollar."

"You do? That's excellent!" you respond as you hold out you hand. "I'll take it now." After a couple of moment's hesitation you say, "Oh, I see. You mean I owe you one dollar. That's right, I do. There's your dollar right there on the floor. It was there long before you picked a card. Please pick up your dollar. Unfold it. What's inside? A playing card? But not just any playing card. It's the Six of Hearts. But not just any Six of Hearts. It's a Six of Hearts with one piece missing. Do you still have that piece of card? Can you please hold the piece up to the card? Does it fit perfectly? It does! That means it's exactly the same Six of Hearts!"

The audience goes wild.

What You Need

✔ A dollar bill
✔ A deck of cards
✔ A duplicate Six of Hearts from a matching deck
✔ Three rubber bands
✔ A bandana
✔ Some double sided tape
✔ An index card 3 inches by 5 inches
✔ A pen
✔ A hardboiled egg
✔ A small paper plate
✔ A saltshaker with a pretty wide opening
✔ A table (or chair, or stool)

What Really Happens

There's a bit of work to do before you can present this to the audience. First gather all the props together. If you don't know how to hardboil an egg, ask an adult for help.

When you have everything together, tear off one corner of one of the Six of Hearts ❶. Don't lose the piece. Fold the card in half and lay it on the middle of the dollar bill ❷. Fold the bill in half, trapping the card in the fold. Fold the dollar in half the other way, really locking in the card ❸.

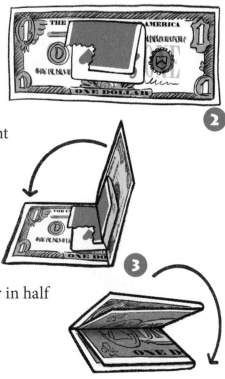

To make the deck that shoots out the Six of Hearts, encircle about 20 cards lengthwise with one of the rubber bands and place this rubber-banded packet sideways on a table 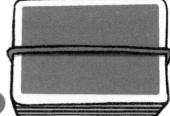. Open them up to the right, like a book, with about 10 cards in each half, stretching out the rubber band **5**. Keeping one hand on the rubber banded cards so that they don't go flying, place the second Six of Hearts face-down onto the left half of the packet **6**. Fold the right half of the packet back over the left half **7**, trapping the Six of Hearts in the middle. This is pretty tricky; the Six wants to shoot out of the left side of the packet—don't let it.

Keeping the newly assembled packet together, insert it into the center of the deck so that there are loose cards above and below the prepared packet. Still keeping a tight grip on the deck (so the Six of Hearts doesn't shoot out), wrap the second rubber band twice around the entire deck from end to end. This keeps everything together until you're ready to perform the trick (**8** reveals all).

The bandana also isn't as innocent as it seems. To prepare it, first cut the index card in half. Set aside one half and fold the other half into eighths. Wrap that folded half card in a piece of double-sided tape so that it's sticky all over and lay the tape-covered card onto one corner of the

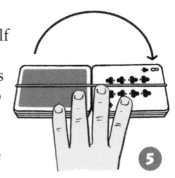

Six of Hearts

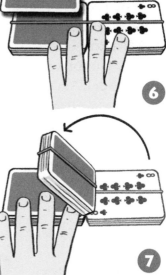

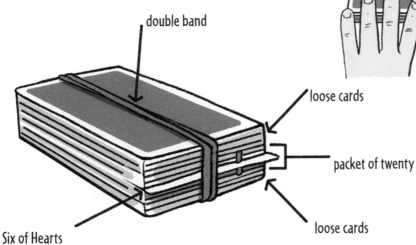

double band

loose cards

packet of twenty

loose cards

Six of Hearts

8

bandana 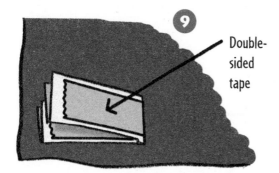. Fold the corner of the bandana over completely concealing the folded index card. Press down on the fabric to ensure it's really stuck to both sides of the folded card .

The other half of the index card will become the I-O-U. Write on it, "I-O-U One Dollar." Fold it up and crease it tightly so that it will fit down into your salt shaker. You want to make sure that its folds won't expand so much that once it's in the salt shaker you can't get it out! Empty all the salt from the shaker, put the I-O-U down inside, and then pour all the salt back in so that the I-O-U is completely buried. Put the cap back on the shaker.

All that remains is to distribute all the props in your pockets so that everything is where you need it. Which reminds me of an excellent hint: It's always a good idea to put your props in exactly the same place each time you perform. That way you can concentrate on the presentation of your tricks instead of having your brain distracted by thoughts like "Hmm. Now where did a put that deck of cards?"

Anywho, put the torn corner of the Six of Hearts in your left front pants pocket. Put the deck with the rubber band around it in that same pocket. The egg goes in your right front pants pocket. On top of the egg put the folded dollar bill (with the card inside). Make sure the folded edge of the dollar is toward the top of your pocket (this makes it a lot easier to pull out without accidentally unfolding it). The plate goes in the small of your back under your shirt with its bottom edge held in the waistband of your pants.

Double-sided tape

Leave the back of your shirt untucked. The salt shaker goes in your right back pocket. ⑪ shows everything in its place. Don't sit down!

Now that you're stuffed with stuff, there's one other little detail to tend to before you're ready to perform. Prior to your performance, fold the bandana up into a pocket-sized rectangle with the card-concealing corner on the inside. Without calling attention to yourself, give it to someone who'll be in your audience and ask him to put it in his pocket. Tell him that during the show he should offer it up when you ask to borrow a handkerchief. By having the bandana already folded and asking him to put it in his pocket you greatly reduce the risk of him opening it prematurely and discovering the secret device in the corner.

Now, finally, you're ready to perform! In the above description of this trick I've spelled out the proceedings and dialogue pretty specifically, so in the explanation that follows I will mainly be detailing the secret actions and giving you the

folded dollar with card inside

deck

plate

egg

corner of
Six of Hearts

salt shaker

11

bare minimum of the actual presentation. Refer to the "What They See" section to get the complete story.

Begin by asking to borrow a dollar. Fold it in quarters, so that it resembles the dollar you have in your pocket. Ask, "Is this the dollar you gave me?" When the person says yes, put the dollar in your pocket saying, "Thank you." As soon as the dollar is in your pocket shift your grip from the borrowed dollar to the prepared dollar, but don't bring it out just yet. Wait for the laughter to stop and then withdraw the prepared dollar and say, "Just kidding. I actually wanted this for a purpose." Fold the dollar one more time so that it's in eighths and put it under the table leg.

After you check the table for stability, face the audience again and ask to borrow a handkerchief. You should be offered the one you planted with an audience member. Take it and make a big production of noisily pretending to blow your nose in it. (Note: It's probably best not to actually blow anything into the bandana.) Decide you like the looks of the bandana and put it in your left back pocket.

Announce that it's time for a card trick and take the deck from your pocket. Keeping pressure on the deck (so the Six of Hearts doesn't shoot out), remove the outer rubber band and place it around your wrist. Maintaining pressure on the deck, slightly fan it out ⑫ and approach a spectator asking them to pick a card. Just as they're about to reach for a card, relax pressure on the deck and the Six of Hearts will shoot forth. There should be a laugh. If you say, "Oh, you dropped it" at the right time the laugh should get bigger.

Six of Hearts ready to shoot out

Placing the deck aside on the table, pick up the Six of Hearts and display it to everyone and then hand it to the person you asked to select a card. Now ask the spectator to tear the card in half. The wording on this request is important, so I'll repeat it here: "We're going to do a very special trick with that card. I know this is going to seem weird, but don't worry, it'll all work out in the end. I want you to tear the card in half . . ." Notice that you are acknowledging that what you are about to ask him to do is odd, but he should do it anyway. This is to get him over his hesitation to ruin a completely good card. You should also make a tearing gesture with your hands as an example of what you want him to do.

As soon as he's torn the card you complete your sentence, "...mentally." This should get a BIG laugh. While the audience is laughing, place both hands into your front pants pockets. As soon as your left hand gets the torn corner of the Six of Hearts into its curled fingers, bring both hands back out. Keep the fingers curled so that no one sees the piece of card. Your left thumb holds the piece of card securely behind your left fingers 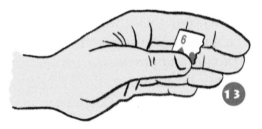. The big laugh focuses attention away from you onto the spectator and provides cover for this secret action.

Keeping the fingers of both hands curled loosely (to help conceal the torn piece in the left hand), demonstrate the action of tearing a card as you ask the spectator to tear the two pieces of card into four, and the four into eight.

Extend your right hand palm up and ask the spectator to drop all eight pieces on your hand. After the spectator dumps all the pieces in your right hand, look him right in the eye and say, "Wait." When you say, "Wait" and look the spectator in his eyes, I guarantee that he will look you in the eyes, too. As soon as he looks away from your right hand, reach up with your left hand (keep it palm-down so they can't see the piece hidden behind your left fingers) and touch your palm down left hand to the pile of pieces on your palm-up right hand 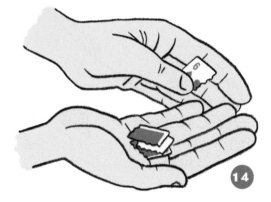.

Turn your left hand palm-up and turn your gaze to the secret extra piece displayed there and say, "You should keep one piece." Hand him the piece in your left hand (it's the one that matches the card in the dollar).

Remove the rubber band from your right wrist and wrap it around the eight pieces of card, making a little bundle, handing it to the spectator.

With your
left hand,
bring out the
bandana and
spread it over
your left hand,
making sure
you arrange
it so that the
corner with the
concealed card
is nearest you.
Take the
rubber-banded

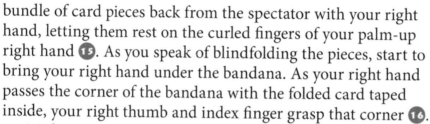

bundle of card pieces back from the spectator with your right
hand, letting them rest on the curled fingers of your palm-up
right hand ⑮. As you speak of blindfolding the pieces, start to
bring your right hand under the bandana. As your right hand
passes the corner of the bandana with the folded card taped
inside, your right thumb and index finger grasp that corner ⑯.

Without pausing, your right hand continues up under the
bandana and pushes the corner of the bandana it's holding
up into the center of the bandana. As soon as you reach the
position shown in ⑰, your left hand withdraws from under
the bandana and moves around to the top of the bandana and
grasps the folded card through the folds of the bandana ⑱.

Your right hand (concealing the rubber banded pieces in
you loosely
closed fingers)
moves from
under the
bandana as
your left hand
holds out the
bandana to
the spectator.
As you ask
the spectator
to grasp the
pieces of card

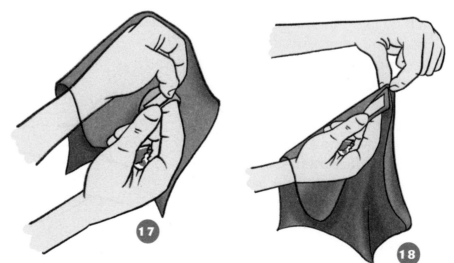

through the bandana, your right hand continues it's downward journey moving toward your right front pants pocket. After the spectator has a good grip on the folded card through the bandana, your left hand lets go. He thinks he's holding the seven rubberband encircled pieces of the Six of Hearts, but you've secretly substituted the folded card concealed in the corner of the bandana.

Then your right hand (with its concealed bundle) goes into your right front pants pocket, lets go of the rubber banded pieces, and comes out of your pocket with the egg, announcing, "An egg."

Congratulations! Once you get to this point you're home free. All the dirty work is done and yet, to the audience, it seems like the trick is really only just beginning.

Say, "Over there the card, over here an egg." Repeat that phrase a couple of times, each time looking more and more closely at the egg. Finally, crack open the egg revealing its hardboiled state. Reach up under the back of your shirt and remove the plate. Peel the egg, placing the pieces of shell on the plate. Reach into your right back pocket and bring forth the salt shaker. Sprinkle a little salt on the peeled egg, set the plate and salt shaker on the table as you focus all of your interest on the egg. Pretend to be completely unaware of the audience watching you as you eat the egg bite by bite.

As you finish devouring the egg you gradually become more conscious of the audience and say, "Oh yes, the card and egg trick." Look at the eggshell pieces and realize that you no longer have an egg. Ask to borrow an egg. When you realize that no one is going to give you an egg, begin to look around for an object to use instead. After a few seconds of glancing hopelessly around, "notice" the saltshaker and announce the "Card and Saltshaker Trick."

Hold up the saltshaker and then grasp one corner of the bandana with you other hand. Ask the person holding the bandana if he can feel the pieces of card inside. After he says that he can, pause a second and then announce, "They're gone!" as you yank the bandana from his grasp. Wave the bandana around, demonstrating its emptiness. Because the folded card remains concealed in the corner it appears that the pieces have vanished!

Toss the bandana aside and slowly unscrew the cap of the saltshaker. Pour the salt onto the plate revealing that there is a folded item amongst the pile of salt. Hold the plate out so the spectator can pick the folded paper out of the mound of salt.

Tell him to open up the paper and ask him if it's a card. When he responds that it is a note, ask him to read it aloud.

He says, "I-O-U one dollar."

In response you of course hold out you hand as you say, "You do? That's excellent! I'll take it now." Pause, and then realizing what he means, you bring the trick to its exciting conclusion by suiting your actions to these words: "Oh, I see. You mean I owe you one dollar. That's right I do. There's your dollar right there on the floor. It was here long before you picked a card. Please pick up your dollar. Unfold it. What's inside? A playing card? But not just any playing card. It's the Six of Hearts. But not just any Six of Hearts. It's a Six of Hearts with one piece missing. Do you still have that piece of card? Can you please hold the piece up to the card? Does it fit perfectly? It does! That means it's exactly the same Six of Hearts!"

BE PREPARED

This trick is kind of a lesson in psychology, because in the description I've really gone into all the details of where you look, and how your actions influence the spectator's actions and help make the trick easier to accomplish and more deceptive. These are the little things that make the difference between a decent performance and a great one. You can do this trick without paying attention to these little details, but the more fine points you include the better your trick will seem to the audience.

If your pockets are full of other props, or you're just uncomfortable with stashing all this stuff on your person, you can have it in a backpack or paper bag, but I just think there's something naturally funny about pulling out an egg, a plate, and a salt shaker from your pockets.

There are a couple of slightly challenging moments in this trick. Let's go over how to defeat those challenges, shall we?

First, depending on where you're doing this trick and who you're doing it for, you might not be able to borrow a dollar, so under some circumstances it might be a good idea to give a dollar to some audience member before the show and tell him that if no one else lends you a dollar, you'll borrow the one you've given him.

Next, when you ask a spectator to tear the card in half, he may be reluctant to actually do so. If he hesitates or asks you a question, you must guide him to do it by saying something like, "Trust me, this will all work out in the end. Just tear the card in half. . . ." and then pause again hoping that they rip the card on this second request. If they still won't do it then you'll probably have to sacrifice the ". . .mentally" gag and just get more explicit. Don't worry about it, it's just a joke and won't affect the trick at all. Whatever you do, don't drag this out by badgering them to tear the card hoping to get a laugh. This only works if for a moment it really seems like you didn't want them to actually tear the card.

This trick is based on one I first learned from Bill Severn, who used to write about magic for *Boy's Life* magazine and who also has a whole bunch of great magic books that are still available. I like it because it's not just a quick trick that's over in a minute. It has a number of situations that are naturally funny without you having to strain to tell jokes. It has a plot with tangents that seem to make no sense, yet everything ends up all tied to together in the end. It makes a mighty satisfying and thoroughly entertaining magical package for your audience.

THE NEXT STEPS

You say you've mastered every amazing trick I've offered up here and you want more? What else can you do to feed your new magic obsession? Here are my suggestions for the next steps to take in making magic your life. . . .

Read More Magic Books

Believe it or not, Scout Magic isn't the only book ever written about the fascinating art of magic. Here are few I'd recommend:

Tricks With Your Head by Mac King and Mark Levy
Mac King's Magic in a Minute Great Big Ol' Book-O-Magic by Mac and Bill King
Learn Magic by Henry Hay
Magic For Dummies by David Pogue
Mark Wilson's Complete Course in Magic by Mark Wilson
The Royal Road to Card Magic by Jean Hugard and Frederick Braue
Any book by Bill Severn or Karl Fulves

Subscribe to a Magic Magazine

That's right, there are whole magazines devoted to your new hobby. Each month they have fantastic articles about famous magicians, and even tricks you can learn. My two favorites are:

Genii Magazine
4200 Wisconsin Ave. NW
Suite 106-384
Washington, DC 20016
www.geniimagazine.com

MAGIC Magazine
6220 Stevenson Way
Las Vegas, NV 89120
www.magicmagazine.com

Join a Magic Club

If you live in a town of any size, chances are there's a club of actual magicians who meet once a month who'd love to have you join them. If so, they're probably affiliated with one (or both) of the two main magic societies in the United States...

SAM (Society of American Magicians)
www.magicsam.com

IBM (International Brotherhood of Magicians)
www.magician.org

More Mac

Campfire Magic is just one part of the phenomenon that is Mac King. Check out www.MacKingShow.com, www.MagicinaMinute.com, and www.MacKingShop.com to learn more great tricks, join the Mac King Fan Club, and to find out more about Mac King and his Magic in a Minute empire.

WHO'S WHO AT MAC KING'S MAGIC IN A MINUTE

Meet the Author

Acclaimed by many as the premiere comedy magician in the world today, Mac King was just named "Magician of the Year" by the Magic Castle in Hollywood, just appeared on his seventh TV special for NBC-TV, just got voted the sixth best show in all of Las Vegas, and just rocked the audience on *The Late Show with David Letterman*. He is currently starring in the long running "The Mac King Comedy Magic Show" at Harrah's Casino and Hotel in Las Vegas. As an after dinner corporate entertainer, he has wowed companies around the world with his astounding sleight of hand and irresistible humor.

Between his World's Greatest Magic TV specials for NBC, his book *Tricks With Your Head*, his made-for-TV Mac King School of Magic, his hilarious line of Magic in a Minute toys, his magic sets *Suitcase-O-Magic, Book-O-Magic,* and *Lunchbox-O-Magic*, and his nationally syndicated comic strip Mac King's *Magic in a Minute*, Mac has probably started more beginners on the road to magic as a hobby than anyone else, ever. And, according to his wife and daughter, he is a fine husband, a great dad, and all around swell fellow.

Meet the Illustrator

Illustrator and graphic designer Bill King was raised in Dunwoody, Georgia, and educated at the University of Mississippi. For many years he designed the little toys that came in cereal boxes. Now he draws Mac King's *Magic in a Minute* comic strip and helps design Mac's toys, books, and magic kits. He also makes periodic visits to Mac's house to clean out his refrigerator and play in his pool. Bill lives in Chicago, Illinois, and is married to the beautiful and talented Joetta. They have two dull-witted cats (Chubby & Minnie) and the greatest dog in the universe (WOODY!).

Meet the Monkey

Lewis T. Monkey is a Brookings fellow, a Nobel Laureate, and holds several PhDs. He lives with his mother, Ida, and sister, Ima, in Simian, Indiana.

Acknowledgements

I didn't invent all the tricks in this book; each one was created by Lewis the Monkey. Actually, of course, a real, live human being invented every trick ever done. This seems obvious, but most people don't ever think of where magic tricks come from. There are people who don't ever perform tricks, they only invent them. There are lots of ways to make magic your hobby. I've had the pleasure of meeting and being friends with some of the finest inventors of magic tricks in the world. Hopefully, one day you'll get to meet some of the people who came up with some of the tricks I've presented here. So, if you come across Max Maven, William Larsen Sr., Mark Levy, Karl Fulves, Brad Ball, Sam Loyd, Mel Stover, Martin Gardner, Michael Weber, David Williamson, Mark Wilson, Mike Caveney, Tina Lenert, Johnny Thompson, Joseph Leeming, Bill Severn, Henry Hay, Jerry Andrus, Todd Karr, Walter Gibson, Karl Fulves, Jack Tillar, Kim Iles, Nick Trost, Bob Hummer, U. F. Grant, Penn and Teller, Lance Burton, Robert David Michaels, Mike Close, Peter Studebaker, George McAthy, Bruce Elliot, Neepy Vernon, Bill Bowman, Bill Herz, Jim Steinmeyer, Monte Johnson, or Lewis the Monkey, please bow down before them and offer a sincere thank you.

In addition to the above list, Bill and I would also like to thank Jennifer, Joetta, Eli, Lew, Linda, Bettye, Cookie, Pax, and Elwood for their love, encouragement and comforting pats on the head.

And then there's Nathaniel Marunas, Jeff Knurek, David Hoyt, Dinah Dunn, Jack Barnette, and Monte Johnson. They're the true brains behind all this, and the real reason any of these *Magic in a Minute* ventures exist.

And finally, the big thank you goes to you. I sure do appreciate you buying the book, and I hope you'll have a whole mess-o-fun with the tricks, and that this leads to a lifetime love of magic.